REASON AND ROMANTICISM

REASON AND ROMANTICISM

Essays in Literary Criticism

By HERBERT READ

Homo est quodammodo omnia
—ST. THOMAS AQUINAS

New York
RUSSELL & RUSSELL
1963

FIRST PUBLISHED IN 1926
REISSUED, 1963, BY RUSSELL & RUSSELL, INC.
L. C. CATALOG CARD NO: 63—15175
PRINTED IN THE UNITED STATES OF AMERICA

CONTENTS

NOTE

CERTAIN of these essays have appeared, sometimes in a slightly different form, in the following periodicals: *The Times Literary Supplement*, *The Criterion*, *The Yale Review*, and *The Dial.* The author desires to express his obligations to the editors of these periodicals.

REASON AND ROMANTICISM

I

THE ATTRIBUTES OF CRITICISM

Une croyance est l'œuvre de notre esprit, mais nous ne sommes pas libres de la modifier à notre gré. Elle est notre création, mais nous ne le savons pas. Elle est humaine et nous la croyons Dieu. Elle est l'effet de notre puissance et elle est plus forte que nous.—FUSTEL DE COULANGES, *La Cité antique*.

§ 1

IN the practice of criticism a writer will habitually isolate certain aspects of his mind, giving a definition and coherence to ideas which are in reality linked or correlated with his complete individuality. If we adopt an image that has been more than once used of the mind, and compare it to a crystal of many facets, then we may say that the literary critic is accustomed to present only one or two facets to the light. The others recede into a shadowy perspective, or disappear altogether as to another hemisphere. Perhaps the complete crystal can only be revealed in a life developed fully in all its instincts and desires—a life, moreover, of active expression, demanding physique and will of an exceptional kind. Such a life (like Goethe's) seems to be admirable only in our theoretic moods: we have a more lively interest in personalities of an uneven grain, in which some faculties are developed at the expense of others, giving a sharp division of light and shade. These personalities (Rousseau, Stendhal, Nietzsche . . .) have a greater effect on the development of thought because of this force of attraction. By their imperfection they appeal to our own faulty make-up, and we can extend to them sympathy, pity, and other humane feelings which really represent in us the empire of fallible instincts. What is more classic and complete leaves us unmoved, in an emotional sense, and is therefore less effective.

But whether the mind is of this classic type, or of the fragmentary romantic type, it is necessary, in criticism, to begin with a concept of unity. The critic must aim to discover some utmost extent of mental territory to which the given expression of the author may be related. Equally, I think, the critic must reveal his own territory. He must contrive to show all the main facets—those which reflect most light in his life. For an opinion or judgment is never uttered except as the offspring of a total attitude. It issues from the inner centre which governs and co-ordinates every facet of the revolving spheroid. A literary judgment, though based on the closest scientific assessment of the objective facts, is not genuine unless coloured by the subjective intention of the originator. A view, not merely of literature, but of life is involved; not merely the science of writing, but also the philosophy of being.

To appreciate the flexible tendency of one's mind—to float with the current of one's likes and dislikes (and that is legitimate enough when the current flows steadily in one direction)—by such means a tolerable body of criticism may be evolved. But there comes a time when it is possible to see the vanity of one's own gesticulations, and then conscience cries Stop! Your particular opinions, given upon every or several occasions, tend to immerse you in their particularity. You have surveyed a long tract, measuring distances, taking angles, making notes: but you have not yet plotted out your map. Each essay is a collection of figures; your country is but a landscape travelled through: it remains to reduce it to an exact chart. Such an ambition may be vain, and in any case there is a dilemma involved. The past of any reasonable man is strewn with dead enthusiasms, and it is quite relevant to ask why one moment should be made more absolute than another. And there is an analogous fear that principles once enunciated may compromise the future. Once shaped out of the fluid consciousness, these personal ideas become rigid and irretrievable, exercising a suggestive power on all future faith, all aptitude for change with the changing times, all motives in a fresh conjunction of events.

These risks are nevertheless taken, firstly because

one acts from impulse in such matters, and then because it is a possible fiction, to say the least of it, that one can in this way approach to a condition of quasi-dogmatism. I hesitate to say dogmatism simply, because that would recall Dr. Johnson, who was anything but a scientific critic; and because there is some truth in Nietzsche's aphorism to the effect that the desire to find laws in nature is the mark of an inferior mind. But, arising out of any serious consideration of the discreet facts of literature, there are certain abstractions which have the aspect of universality, and I take it that it is the function of the critic to define these abstractions and by so doing establish a tradition which in some way or other is superior to the facts.

But, with these reservations, let us speak of dogmas, which are articles of faith. Faith is attained by a long process of experience, and without this rationale of experience, confessions of faith are difficult to make. They are not only difficult to express, because they demand clarity and concision if they are not to be abused, but they are also difficult to receive, representing as they do our most intransigent moods. Faith is aggressive, supercilious, and often priggish: it arouses resentment because it is a standpoint reached, a certain definite attainment, beyond deviation or compromise.

The positing of dogmas, whether concerning life or literature, seems to me the only considerable business of criticism. Dogmas are the only solidities among successive and inconstant waves of appreciation and amorphous sensibility. The fear that dogmas infringe liberty should not deter us for a moment, for the final object of criticism is the criticism of dogma, and only those dogmas which express values above and beyond liberty need or will survive the assaults of the critical spirit.

§ 2

Perhaps I can best state my own views by taking up a position, in the military sense, facing another critic's faith. In an essay called "For a Declaration of War", Mr. Waldo Frank[1] gives us the fullest and most radical expression of a critical attitude that I know. This attitude I believe to have different values for the unstable culture of America, to which it is addressed, than for the complex traditions of European culture. It is from the standpoint of the latter culture that I examine it here.

It will be necessary to quote somewhat extensively from Mr. Frank's essay in order to be quite fair to it. Here is the preliminary statement of his case:

"There has been then for the entire term of History in the Western world a common culture: a common Whole. The matrix of this whole was a group of spiritual and intellectual convictions.

[1] *Salvos*, 1924.

In this matrix, the man of religion and the artist worked, and from it the peoples looked out upon the world. Here, with no attempt at thoroughness, are some of these convictions:

"1. Unity is truth. This is a universe, not a multiverse.
2. Earth is the most important part of the universe. Sun and stars revolve around it.
3. Man is lord of the world of creature. He is physical life's highest and ultimate expression.
4. Man's reason is autonomous.
5. Man's conception of reality is fundamentally correct. This is so
   a. Because the senses tell the truth;
   b. or because reason corrects the senses;
   c. or because God (Wisdom) supplements the senses and co-operates with reason.
6. God (or Gods, unified by the Greeks as well as by the Hebrews) is good and is related to man's experience.
7. The exercise of reason tends towards happiness.
8. The exercise of virtue tends toward blessedness.
9. We know what is good and what is evil.
10. We know what matter is, even if we cannot define it.
11. We know what thought is, even if we cannot define it.
12. Time and space are what they seem to be.
13. Energy and matter are indestructible.

14. The Law of cause and effect, upon which logic rests, is absolute.
15. A man may be builded of myriad individuals . . . electrons, atoms, cells, monads, etc. But man himself is not such a particle. There are no individuals of which the *instantaneous* individual man is possibly a cellular, atomic, or relational part.
16. Intellect is three-dimensional: and life is three-dimensional.

" These basal assumptions had various forms. Some lands stressed some of them, some epochs ignored others. Many of them were rejected by individuals whose revolt, however, did not adumbrate in the experience of the race. They provide a rough estimate of the matrix within which civilization was born, and of the foundations in which it was reared and nurtured. Thinkers, poets, scientists, and priests established them. Through the aesthetic experience and the religious dogma they based the experience, however unconsciously, of billions of men and women.

" They are breaking up.

" The process of their destruction, *i.e.*, of the destruction of the spiritual and experiential whole which their acceptance meant, left the sporadic and entered the organic state with such men as Copernicus, Bacon, Descartes, Spinoza. In the Nineteenth Century the process accelerated vastly. With such forces as Kant, Schopenhauer, Darwin, Kelvin, Freud, the Non-Euclidean and *n*-dimensional mathematicians and with the apposite introduction into Europe of Hindu religious ideas which have always been based upon a deeper unity, the destructive work, *on the intellectual plane*, was practically rounded.

* * *

" The reader who is at all aware will know that not a single one of these basal convictions has been spared, *except the first*. And the first is the categorical imperative of any culture, the expression of the social will to survive."

I think we shall find it possible to accept the whole of Mr. Frank's analysis of modern western culture and its intellectual break-up, and yet to deny the conclusions he draws from it. For the description of this break-up of intellectual concepts is made to lead to an assumption of the break-up of the European tradition itself, and, as a corollary, to the assumption of a new consciousness in America which is destined to replace these dying values.

The vital presupposition in Mr. Frank's hypothesis is made in the first sentence of the passage quoted. It is not true to say that there has been a common culture for the entire term of history in the western world. There have been at least two such cultures: the pre-Renaissance and the post-Renaissance. Mediaeval philosophy, like modern science, would deny most of the sixteen intellectual convictions in Mr. Frank's list. Mr. Frank's mistake is to imagine there is anything strange in the modern attitude. It is possible to show historically that an opposition between two such sets of cultural values has always existed, and that it corresponds to deep-rooted psychological orientations which from time to time alternate in their dominance. It would take us too far from our immediate object to explain this opposition in detail, but it is an opposition reflected in all forms of sensibility: in the opposition between natural and transcendental religions, between representational and non-representational art, between humanistic and absolute philosophies, between idealistic and realistic politics. The opposition is perhaps in the end to be traced to material and economic factors, such as the contrast between the seeming friendliness of nature in a southern climate and the seeming aggressive terror of nature in a northern climate. It has its microcosmic aspect or analogue in the individual, particularly in the distinction between the extraverted and introverted types. But whether as an emotional, intellectual, or economic opposition, it is entirely disregarded by Mr. Frank, and the fundamental unsoundness of his position is due to this lapse.

The tradition of the northern European or Germanic races is, in its emotional aspects, the Gothic tradition—transcendental religion, non-representational art and a non-humanistic philosophy. Intellect, because of its logical, fixed, and universal nature, is not subject to the same differentiations; the emotions respond to environment, but the intellect defeats it. The philosophy of Aristotle may owe some of its concreteness to its Aryan racial origins; in any case it was, by reason of its intellectual cast, easily absorbed into the emotional attitude of the Gothic spirit. In this way scholasticism became the intellectual correlative of Gothic art, and the first European tradition reached its perfect expression in the thirteenth century. The tradition with which Mr. Frank is occupied is quite another tradition; it has its origins in a different emotional attitude, and this attitude has its own expression in art and its own rationalization in philosophy: it has the Renaissance, the Humanists, and the Cartesians, in fact.

It may be that Mr. Frank would urge that the Renaissance culture carries with it its economic background, and that not only the culture, but also the economic structure, has run its course; and that everything else is involved thereby. To this I would reply:

(*a*) That America is part of the same economic structure and is equally involved in any catastrophe. This would dispose of any special pleading on behalf of American culture. But I would rather argue:

(*b*) That culture is to a great extent independent of *social* changes, as distinct from basic *economic* needs. The resources of Europe, in materials, in racial energy, in knowledge, show no signs of not being equal to these basic economic needs. The social structure of Imperial Russia has disappeared: its economic resources remain; so, under different aspects, does its culture. So would, under a similar transformation, the culture of Europe in general.[1]

I cannot help suspecting that Mr. Frank has been misled by what Professor Irving Babbitt, an American who does not despise European culture, has called America's "frontier psychology". "We in this country have received a peculiar psychic twist from the fact that we have had endless elbow-room. A chief danger both to ourselves and others is that we shall continue to have a frontier psychology long after we have ceased to have a frontier. For a frontier psychology is expansive, and expansiveness, I have tried to show, is, at least in

[1] Another answer is possible, which, however, I do not prefer to use: it is not so absolute. But as expressed by Havelock Ellis it is a very possible retort to Mr. Frank. "As a civilisation declines in brutal material energy it gains in spiritual refinement, thus winning more subtle and permanent influence. . . . In the very dying down of these grosser energies there is hope, for we may be sure that the forces of life are not yet extinct, and that worthier and subtler ends will float before our eyes as the sculleries and outhouse offices of life are gradually removed elsewhere. England, there can be little doubt, is peculiarly fitted to exercise the finer functions of civilisation, if not indeed for the world generally, at all events for those peoples of the globe which are allied to her wholly by language and largely by race. In new countries, in the hurry of cities, in the barren solitude of plains and hills, men have no time or no chance to elaborate the ideals and visions for which they yet thirst; they are not in touch with those great traditions on which alone all worthy and abiding effort must finally rest" (*Affirmations*, 2nd ed., 1915, p. 229).

its political manifestations, always imperialistic."[1] Mr. Frank has shown that it can be equally imperialistic in its spiritual manifestations.

It is typical of Mr. Frank's misunderstanding of the European tradition that he should regard as part of the destructive work which has been completed against our "dying culture", "the apposite introduction into Europe of Hindu religious ideas", and he shows generally a sympathy towards oriental religiosity. This again, I would say, indicated a fundamental misunderstanding of the European tradition—a misunderstanding which in this respect he shares with the more portentous Keyserling.[2] The one tendency that emerges from all Count Keyserling's observations and experiences may best be expressed by the word *orientalism*. This appears not as a direct advocacy of the philosophies of the East, but implicitly, from their standpoint, as a reflection on the adequacy of Western thought. But this comparison is only made effective by ignoring one half—and that the most significant half—of Western thought. Like Mr. Frank, Keyserling identifies Western thought with that particular subjectivist trend of which he is the outcome. Now this particular trend sees the East through rose-coloured spectacles: its peculiar heresies are of Eastern origin, or at any rate

[1] *Democracy and Leadership*, by Irving Babbitt, 1924, p. 240.

[2] See especially *The Travel Diary of a Philosopher*, by Count Hermann Keyserling, translated by J. Holroyd Reece. London, 1925.

derive a great deal of encouragement from the East. Let us recall Schopenhauer's claim on behalf of his master: "It was reserved for Kant to carry victoriously into Europe and its philosophy that profound idealistic vision common to all Asia apart from Islam, and dominating its very religion". If we were required to point to a philosophy worked out in the terms of Western reality and consonant with our deepest instincts, we should turn to mediaeval philosophy and particularly to the thought of St. Thomas Aquinas. That is not to say so much as that we shall find in St. Thomas a Western philosophy for all time; but we shall find there an attitude and a method more fruitful for our purposes than those of Buddha or Confucius. And it may be suggested that our efforts, and especially the efforts of our philosophers, could with more profit be turned towards an elucidation of the content and an interpretation of the system of scholasticism than towards these idle "adventures of the soul" among oriental mystics. Henri Massis,[1] who perhaps best expresses in France a very natural opposition to this trend of orientalism, has observed: "Le caractère de l'Occident, c'est la *distinction*; et le programme de la pensée occidentale est assez bien rassemblé, dès les hautes époques, par la sentence classique d'Anaxagore: 'Au début tout était confondu;

[1] In an excellent symposium on the subject published in *Les Cahiers du Mois*, nos. 9-10, "Les Appels de l'Orient", p. 36. Paris (Emile-Paul), 1925.

l'intelligence vint et mit chaque chose en ordre'. C'est de la vue de cet ordre, des hiérarchies intellectuelles qu'il comporte, de la vue des ressemblances et des différences, des identités et des distinctions, que résulte, par un processus à la fois rationnel et naturel, ce mouvement général, et, en particulier, ce développement de la *personne humaine* qui frappe, dès l'abord, dans l'histoire de l'Occident."

All this Keyserling ignores, and in his ignorance he is true to his race; for if his immediate origins are as near the shallows as Houston Stewart Chamberlain, they reach without intermission right back to the profounder depths of Kant. To deny the objective reality of the content of knowledge can only lead to this now too familiar cult of the self—to this gospel of inwardness, to this denial of the validity of science, to "the ideal of personal perfection as opposed to that of professional efficiency". But from these particular falsities Mr. Frank is presumably free, for I think he would see how intimately linked they are with the dying culture he is discarding. The most distressing aspect of Keyserling's book is its aimlessness. "Europe has nothing more to give me. Its life is too familiar to force my being to new developments . . . I want to let the climate of the tropics, the Indian mode of consciousness, the Chinese code of life and many other factors, which I cannot envisage in advance, work their spell upon me one after the other, and then watch what will become of me." A mind so "willing" meets a common fate. Lacking any objective standard of judgment, it is seduced by every profundity it encounters. As he goes on his way, Count Keyserling surrenders himself to every spiritual nostrum in turn, unconscious of any loss of dignity entailed. Thus Theosophy and Buddhism, New Thought and Confucianism, Mormonism and Catholicism, are all treated with the same ponderous enthusiasm. Mr. Frank is more positive. He has a mind of his own, and for the fifteen defunct convictions of a moribund Europe he offers us fourteen articles of a new creed of which Art is the ineffable Logos.

§ 3

In one sense our condition (but not only *our* condition, but the condition of the whole western world) is hopeless enough. We have carried criticism to the last degree of scepticism, even to the point where it becomes sceptical of itself, and have yet no new synthesis. We have destroyed our religion, and have left the emotions without a control. Emotions—which are individual, disparate, and therefore contradictory—must be disciplined in a social community. The function of religion has always been the absorption and unification of emotions—the real and essential identity of the Many in the One.

That the critical spirit, expressed in reason, will

ever evolve a synthesis capable of fulfilling the functions of religion is evidently impossible. Reason and emotion only unite in very rare and special perceptions; such perceptions are not capable of generalization. Emotions are too diffuse, too widely distributed, ever to be unified in reason, which is an evolved possession, never perfect at all, and only approaching perfection in rare individuals. But the negativeness of reason, in this sense, does not imply the reintegration of the old sacred concepts. The criticism of revealed religion has been operative not only on the empirical plane (which matters little) but also on the psychological plane. A religion like Christianity is built up largely of unconscious symbols: it finds its most powerful forces in subconscious processes, like prayer, grace, and faith. The effect of experimental science has been to destroy the unconsciousness of these symbols: it understands them and therefore equates them with conscious equivalents, which are no longer symbols and which on that account no longer compel the imagination.[1]

Mr. Waldo Frank, in the essay referred to, after an analysis of the culture of the western world which I have shown to be true only so far as it goes, proceeds to an assumption which is wholly false. He argues that because the forces of intellect have destroyed our only unity, which was religious, that therefore the *form* of our life is decomposing. He seems to make an identity

[1] *Cf.* p. 106.

between the forms of life and religious experience which is of doubtful validity. Religion is expressed in dogma; but intellect is an energy. It seems to me futile to say that because that energy has destroyed the dogmas, that therefore it has destroyed itself. It proceeds, rather, to the creation of new dogmas. But, objects Mr. Frank, "Science has negatively proven what philosophy, which can prove nothing, stated. Science has done this after a complacent period of positivism in which it ignored the intuitions of the poets and the statements of the philosophers who had declared in a hundred tongues and in a hundred ways the disability of positive science logic to enter the domain of the *noumenal*: the disqualification of positive science from any contact with causes. But this past arrogance of science is found to-day only among journalists and pedagogues who are always at least a century behind the times. The study of a Poincaré or of an Einstein is pure of it. Positive science has achieved its greatest dignity in the admission of Nescience: the admission of Mystery as the circumambient limit. It has prepared the intellect to receive Mystery, but it does not itself understand what Mystery is."

My objection to this statement of the outcome of science is mainly concerned with the use of words, or rather with the implication of ideas of which there is no precise expression. Mr. Frank introduces the word *mystery* quite arbitrarily as a synonym for *nescience*. But there is a very fundamental distinction: nescience is a negative word, merely implying an unknown area of knowledge or experience. Mystery, on the other hand, is a very positive word, implying a *quality* in that unknown area—a quality at once irrational and superrational: immanent, but beyond apprehension.

It is necessary to be quite plain on this issue: modern science, dissociating itself from nineteenth-century science, has undoubtedly declared its disability to "enter the domain of the noumenal: the disqualification of positive science from any contact with causes".[1] This does not imply, however, that when science is disqualified, art or religion or any other function of the human mind can step in *as the equivalent* of the scientific method. It merely says: science cannot *know*; art or religion may *guess*. This limits, not the sphere of science, but the scope of the intellect. But it is mere superstition to imagine that what cannot be known in the mind and by intellectual symbols may be apprehended in some other indefinite way. It is mysticism in its most illogical form—mysticism which pretends to be, not merely an alternative to scientific truth (and therefore under certain conditions an acceptable mysticism) but something more inclusive of reality than the scientific method.[2]

[1] The most convincing and at the same time destructive analysis of materialism that I know is to be found in *The Concept of Nature*, by Professor A. N. Whitehead, Sc.D., F.R.S. (1920). See especially pp. 71-3.

[2] There is a saying of Bossuet's which may be recalled here:

Mr. Frank may hold this latter belief, or he may be merely using a word in a loose manner. In any case we must wait for more actual proofs. Mr. Frank assures us that Mystery is not ineffable; that what is ineffable is " conventionalized language—a set of symbols which have crystallized a consciousness smaller than the experience attained by man ". Art is to supply the defect, to be the language of this new consciousness, its first expression in concrete terms. Art can indeed suggest—can *guess* at what lies beyond scientific facts, which admittedly do not account for everything, or for enough. That is the highest function of art, and always has been. But I find it difficult to visualize an art that will " guess " in any manner so utterly divorced from traditional concepts as Mr. Frank seems to foreshadow. I find it difficult to imagine how the great artists of the future will differ from the great artists of the past—from Aeschylus, Dante, El Greco, Bach, Blake, Spinoza, and Whitman, to take Mr. Frank's own selection of names. The religious basis, which I agree with Mr. Frank in recognizing as the common element in these and in all " great primal artists ", is a fairly constant quality for any condition of the human consciousness. The difference between Aeschylus and Whitman is measurable, is almost negligible. I cannot think that in essentials the difference

"True mysticism is so rare and unessential and false mysticism is so common and dangerous that one cannot oppose it too firmly." Quoted by Irving Babbitt, *op. cit.*, p. 260.

between these artists and the artists of the future will be any greater. The state of cultural transition in which we exist is no greater nor more fundamental than several the world has experienced.

Art must conquer new forms of life, and for this purpose art will need new symbols; that is the final declaration of Mr. Frank's faith. But these forms and symbols will emerge parallel with the general development of human thought. It is not likely that this development will take the form of a mystical divorce from reason; or that it will be independent of a continuance of the traditional or "formed phenomena of intellect and sense".

In a way I regret having to controvert, even to this extent, Mr. Frank's position; it is so urgent, so fearless, so straightforward. But it would lead ultimately, I think, to untenable superstitions and a nebulous art. The critical spirit has gained so much, after all these years, in clarity, precision, truth itself, that it is a pity to go back on it merely because it has left us, for the present, in such a naked condition of misery and chaos. We need to create a new unity, or perhaps to recover an old one. But if the critical spirit cannot give us this, no other force will, for that spirit is the highest and most perfected function in man. *No other force will*: that is a large assumption, based on a faith in the consistent development of the human faculties. But these, I recognize, are at the mercy of material chance, and what has not been achieved by the process of thought over many centuries may once again be brought about by a specific event—by the emergence of an individual capable of creating symbols which appeal freshly to the unconscious needs of the mind.

§ 4

Instead of this nebulous and visionary creation of "dimensions of life beyond the scope of its fixed symbols (language)" and the conquest of these new forms of life by the instrumentality of an unimaginable art, I prefer to believe in an art which is the incorporation and enlightening of the ground gained by the intelligence. The critical spirit is not essentially negative or destructive; it can co-exist with the creative spirit, and indeed what is the meaning of this misused word "creative" if it does not connote a discarding of the false as well as a discovery of the true? Art is not an invention in vacuo; it is rather a selection from chaos, a definition from the amorphous, a concretion within the "terrible fluidity" of life. The critical spirit has broken down many false idols, inadequate dogmas, and useless superstitions of age-long force; and such things are more easily destroyed than replaced, so that we are left for the moment a little destitute of comfort. But intelligence is a growing principle in humanity, and an excellent carapace for tender hearts. It not only shelters the growth of the spirit, but trains it to unexpected fertility. All progress is a question of deliberate preparation: the building of foundations, the accumulation of knowledge, the careful cultivation of traditions, and the embodiment of these in institutions. And always discipline and order, with utmost clarity of statement and honesty of thought. It would be better to sacrifice art altogether than to make it a mere anomalous groping into the void of Nescience.

Clarity of statement may require a certain modesty. Instead of cloudy abstractions like Art and Life, it is better to deal in actual attributes. It is the purpose of this book to study such realities in their literary aspect. And in this preliminary essay I wish to define the actual attributes of criticism. I have, I hope, cleared some of the ground by proposing a standpoint more actual and more historically congruous than that of Mr. Waldo Frank. We have now to come closer to the actual texture or type of the critical mind. This, in its ideal accommodation, I would like to identify with the universal mind.

It has been a common saying, since Pope first said it, that a little learning is a dangerous thing. But far more dangerous is the learning which, though not little, is limited. It is idle to think that any good can come of a specialization that is not linked to some wider ethos, itself the product of a versatile intelligence, or that is not subordinate to general wisdom. And this applies not only to the scientist whom we regard rather rashly as the only specialist, but equally to the critic and the poet. A general idea, whether it be a new image or a new hypothesis, invariably springs across two hitherto widely separated concepts: it is the electric spark that plays suddenly *before* contact is made between approaching poles of magnetism. Only a universal mind is likely to contain these pairs of opposites, and for that single reason (and apart from the question of general wisdom) the universal mind alone is capable of "creative" thought. It may be said that this is an impossible ideal: that the rare occurrence of a universal mind, as in Aristotle, Dante, Leibniz, or Goethe, is the definite result of a *lusus naturae*—of chance, in fact. But the universal mind is not necessarily of this order, and universality is a quality possessed by all the rarer spirits of any age: it is a quality I would ascribe, not merely to Aristotle and Leibniz, but to Lucian, Diderot, and Ruskin, as well as to Emily Brontë. It does not mean the possession of all knowledge, or even, necessarily, of any knowledge at all. It does imply a capacity *to receive* all knowledge and events with equanimity and unprejudiced percipience; and to build up a positive attitude on this clear and serene perceptual basis.

This insistence on a positive attitude implies a consciousness of values: it implies a scale. The elucidation of the concept of value is mainly a psychological question, and one that still waits to be properly stated. Mr. Richards, in his *Principles of Literary Criticism*,[1] has attempted to solve the

[1] *Principles of Literary Criticism*, by I. A. Richards. London, 1925.

question in purely realistic terms. Thus " anything is valuable which will satisfy an appetency without involving the frustration of some equal or *more important* appetency. . . . Thus, morals become purely prudential, and ethical codes merely the expression of the most general scheme of expediency to which an individual or a race has attained ". The artist thus becomes an adept in the organization of his impulses, and in the adequate communication of this organization. " His experiences, those at least which give value to his work, represent conciliations of impulses which in most minds are still confused, intertrammelled, and conflicting. His work is the ordering of what in most minds is disordered."

My only objection to this theory is that it results in an ethics of expediency, whereas my experience tells me that an ethical code is an imaginative and perhaps an irrational vision of conduct. It is an immediate or direct apprehension by the intelligence, and not the work of the discursive reason. This distinction, which was established by mediaeval philosophy, I have briefly alluded to in the essay on Pure Poetry (p. 66), and any further expansion of the theme, short of an excursus on the scholastic psychology, is impossible here. It must be sufficient to say that the *value* of a work of art, of a poem equally as of a painting, consists not merely in the progressive organization of the impulses for freedom and fullness of life (Mr. Richards' definition), but also of the open recognition of a moral sanction which is, in the old phraseology, *revealed* to the artist. This process of revelation will also one day, I think, submit to psychological explanation, and perhaps already the method of psycho-analysis and the new *Gestalt* theory of psychology could justify this claim for the direct apprehension of values. In any case an adequate criticism must account for a duality in art—for the presence, in every complete work of art, of ethical values and aesthetic communication. It is a distinction between visualization and significance, and from this point of view has been well expressed by a French writer for whom I have a considerable, if discriminating, respect:

" Les beaux-arts visent à produire, par l'objet qu'ils font, la joie ou la délectation de l'intelligence moyennant l'intuition du sens; (le but de la peinture, disait Poussin, est la délectation). Cette joie n'est pas la joie de l'acte même de connaître, joie de savoir, joie de vrai. C'est une joie qui déborde de cet acte, quand l'objet sur lequel il porte a une proportion excellente à l'intelligence.

" Ainsi cette joie suppose qu'on connaît, et plus il y aura de connaissance, ou de choses données à l'intelligence, plus vaste sera la possibilité de joie; c'est pourquoi l'art en tant qu'ordonné à la Beauté ne s'arrête pas, du moins lorsque son objet le lui permet, aux formes ni aux couleurs, ni aux sons ni aux mots pris en eux-mêmes et *comme choses*, mais il les prend aussi comme faisant connaître autre chose qu'eux, c'est-à-dire *comme signes*. Et la chose signifée peut être signe à son tour, et plus l'objet d'art sera chargé de signification (mais de signification, spontanée et intuitivement saisie, non de signification hiéroglyphique), plus vaste et plus riche et plus haute sera la possibilité de joie et de beauté. La beauté d'un tableau ou d'une statue est ainsi incomparablement plus riche que celle d'un tapis, d'un verre de Venise ou d'une amphore."[1]

M. Maritain is here mainly concerned with the art of painting, but his distinction is equally applicable to the art of writing, and there is no more to say on the matter. Poetry, in short, is delectation, and this delectation is something that surpasses joy in the music of words or delight in images, for words and images reverberate according to the quality of our knowledge, and the greater our knowledge, the more surcharged it is with the perception of values, the deeper will be the delight aroused in us. Art thus only gives joy in proportion to the understanding we bring to it, and our understanding must be of the most universal and sympathetic kind.[2]

§ 5

Finally, there is the dilemma usually posed under the simple terms of *head* and *heart*, but really

[1] *Art et Scolastique*, by Jacques Maritain. Paris, 1920, pp. 79-83.

[2] "Die Welt hat sich realiter zum Menschen emporgebildet, der Mensch soll es idealiter zur Welt". Max Scheler, *Die Formen des Wissens und die Bildung*. Bonn, 1925, p. 12.

involving a very complex and subtle psychological problem. In stating this problem we must try to keep to definite terms. A scientific critic would naturally, in the course of his practice, cite reason as a final criterion. Reason is a very difficult word to use without confusion. It is often used as a synonym for rationality, or even for a mechanistic logic. Reason should rather connote the widest evidence of the senses, and of all processes and instincts developed in the long history of man. It is the sum total of awareness, ordained and ordered to some specific end or object of attention. But obviously this element of order implies duration—it is a system constructed in time and operating in time. It seems needless, on the other hand, to deny that instantaneous type of judgment which we call intuition (*Apriorieinsicht*). In action, when instincts (or habitual reactions) are rapidly roused under the stress of danger or some other emotion, the mind can act without consciousness of its rational background; and act with precision and perfect rightness. I must not be led, at this point, into a discussion of the nature of instinctive judgments: I will only state, as my personal belief, that the *quality* of such judgments is determined by the previous rational training and equipment of the subject acting—in so far as such judgments are of more than immediate value to the consciousness. The majority of them are mere animalistic impulses.

But to return to the practice of criticism. There is in such a ratiocinative process little opportunity for the exercise of intuition. But people will be found to defend, under the shelter of this vague faculty, an emotional attitude which is not without its value. Literature is, after all, mainly an expression of emotional states. I would say it is mainly the control of them. But emotion is the original substance of all aesthetic forms, for even intellectual forms cannot have value as art until they have been emotionally apprehended.

The danger is, that the critical faculty, elaborating its laws too far from its immediate object, may construct categories or ideals which are in the nature of impassive moulds. The critic then returns to the plastic substance of art and in a moment, in the name of science, he has presented us with a rigid shape which he would persuade us is the living reality. But obviously it is dead; it no longer pulses with that life and variability which we ascribe to emotional facts.[1]

[1] *Cf.* Ramon Fernandez, "Le Classicisme de T. S. Eliot", *La Nouvelle Revue Française*, no. 137 (1st February 1925), p. 249: "Le jugement critique implique un effort de définition et de distribution objective qui nous aide à surmonter et à corriger l'état de plaisir indéfinissable. Bien. Mais où nous ne sommes plus guidés par un plaisir immédiat et impérieux (j'entends le plaisir d'un juge cultivé et qui prétend à la compétence), nous risquons de l'être uniquement par une représentation idéale; nous risquons de substituer cette représentation à la réalité esthétique; d'où confusion nouvelle, pour le moins aussi grave que l'autre, car nous inclinerons à mettre une œuvre médiocre qui présentera les caractères que nous avons définis, au-dessus d'une œuvre éminente d'où ces caractères seront absents."

To guard against this false method, the critic has to maintain an attitude which we must describe in another metaphor. He is a man who has carefully elaborated a few dogmas, in the sure belief that without such fixed points no course can be steered, no height measured, and no distances maintained. But having fixed his points, he does not stand still; he is impelled in some direction, and the force that drives him is feeling or emotion. That is the final test of criticism: that its methods are perfected in science, but that the motives are spontaneous, impulsive—aspects of courage, constancy, and devotion. The real act is instantaneous, and the course of history is directed not so much by foresight as by insight.

II

THE NATURE OF METAPHYSICAL POETRY

An examination of the many diverse theories of poetry current since the romantic revival of a hundred years ago would reveal unanimity on one point at least. Rhetoric and thought have been expended, often with ingenious results, on the manner and style of poetry—on questions of the necessity of metre and rhyme, on the relative merits of the ode and sonnet, and on such external subjects as the propriety of realism or the ethical confusions of romanticism. But the poetry thus generously treated approximates in every case to that type known as the lyric; if it is not exactly a lyric, it is a " lyrical passage " from some other kind of poem. In short, poetry has been identified with lyricism. There is, of course, a very good reason for this universal confusion, and my first intention is to make it distinct.

The etymological significance of the word *lyric* is largely lost, but generally it now connotes that quality in writing which we may for the moment be content to call " emotional ". A lyric poem has in addition certain formal characteristics, such as brevity, simplicity, and directness, and for this reason it is commonly held that a good poem cannot be long, or that a long poem can only be good " in parts ". It may further be noted that those poems the world agrees to call lyrical are exclusively concerned with the record of sensibility—of direct sensibility, as in " The Solitary Reaper ", or of those vaguer reactions of direct sensibility that are " the bliss of solitude ". Some lyric poets are sensible of the beauty of the actual phenomenon, others are sensible of the ideal associations of phenomena. But they agree, and it is essential to bear this in mind, in deriving their emotions from a direct awareness of the world—of its women, its flowers, its atmospheres, and its subtleties.

The occasionality of such emotional awareness has resulted in the practice, and then in the theory, of an emotional unity in the poem. An emotion is fleeting and must be seized in its uniqueness; all elements that do not contribute to its expression must be rigorously excluded: clarity, succinctness, simplicity—these are the virtues of the lyric, and, in modern minds, of all poetry. All the elaborate rules, and even all the revolts against any rules, exemplified in modern poetry, have their origin in the peculiar needs of the lyric.

The occasionality of the lyric does not, however, deprive it of a more general utility; a lyric is simply a perception, and all thought is based primarily on perceptions. From the accumulation of selected perceptions, expressed as lyrics, it is obvious that a general view of life may be constructed, and this general view may possess great ethical and aesthetic value. But it will remain a view, a *Weltanschauung*; it cannot become metaphysical until it is converted into concepts. But, in the mind of the modern theorist, to convert perceptions (*i.e.*, emotional perceptions) into concepts is to destroy their poetic quality. In reality, however, such a result is by no means inevitable.

Let us examine more carefully the use of the word *emotion* in this connection. I gather from the critics who have established the lyrical standard of poetry that they use the word in its general psychological sense. Even in psychology any exact scientific use of the word is difficult, as McDougall has shown;[1] and while our critics do not normally expect poetry to embody or inspire primary emotions like anger or fear, the emotions they do demand of poetry differ in degree rather than in kind from these. The tenderness expressed and induced by a lyric may even be so influential as to cause a "lump in the throat", even as fear is accompanied by certain visceral disturbances; and physiology may yet identify and classify the various glandular excretions and their appropriate lyrical responses. Nor am I disposed to deny that the state of attention or contemplation induced by metaphysical poetry may not also have its basis in some material agitation of the human cortex or glandular system. But the business of the literary critic is to identify the mental rather than the

[1] *Social Psychology*, chap. iii.

physiological significance of the material in his hands, and in this sense a more useful distinction can be made in the content of the emotions; though immediately we desert the field of a material science we are driven to the use of inexact terms. But terms are inexact only because they mean different things to different people: to those who are willing to understand, they can convey an exact meaning; and, when I contrast the abstract and the concrete contents of emotions, I do not thereby imply that an abstract content is something vague and indefinable. To the scientific poet, as to the scientific philosopher, abstract conceptions have their exactitudes. With this understanding, I may distinguish the concrete character of the content of the lyric, which in its purest state is concerned with the direct awareness of phenomenal environment, from the abstract character of what I am going to call metaphysical poetry.

Metaphysical poetry is abstract because, like metaphysics, it deals with concepts. But, as poetry, it is no less "emotional" than lyrical poetry—though, since the emotion is differently manifested, it is a question whether that state of vivid contemplation inspired by metaphysical poetry had not better be described by another word. For my present purpose I do not think so, for it is necessary at all costs to maintain a nexus between lyrical poetry and metaphysical poetry in the word *poetry*; and since I despise all distinctions based on the technique or *décor* of poetry, I prefer to justify this nexus in the word *emotion*, which denotes a common foundation in physical fact. Later I shall illustrate the actual character of metaphysical poetry. For the present I will define it as the emotional apprehension of thought—or, to use words suggested by Dante, as thought transmuted into vision:

> e il pensamento in sogno transmutai.

But first it is necessary to indicate certain misconceptions, the most important of which is to imagine that metaphysical poetry is didactic, *and nothing but didactic*, in the deadest sense of the word. It is assumed that metaphysical poetry is the writing of metaphysics or science in the manner of verse, and that while as such it may be a wonderful display of technical virtuosity, it is not poetry in the strict (that is, the lyrical) sense of the word; and some frankly didactic poem, such as *The Botanic Garden* of Erasmus Darwin, is given as an illustration. Lucretius and Dante are slighted by implication. Now it is very difficult to dissociate the idea of didacticism from the idea of metaphysical poetry, but it is essential to any understanding of the subject that this should be done. *The Botanic Garden* is didactic and is not poetry; the *Commedia* is didactic and is poetic. Can we completely disengage the two ideas and say, for instance, that the didacticism of the *Commedia* has nothing at all in common with its poetry? The question is clearer when it is made more general: when it is said, for example, that the *art* of the Middle Ages was didactic.[1] In this case we do not mean that didacticism was of the essence of art; we only mean that the artists of the Middle Ages, urged perhaps by their own religious consciousness, and certainly by the consciousness of their religious environment, inevitably expressed themselves in religious subjects. The result was didactic, but was the process? Surely the process was simply one of *feeling*—of feeling for the significance of the subject in hand—and rarely one of purpose. The purpose perhaps only existed in the minds of the ecclesiastical syndicate that ordered the general design of a cathedral: the artists executed their orders with quite a different intention. In the same way the design of a poem may be didactic, and the fact that design and execution are alike the work of one mind does not alter the fact that aesthetically they may be distinct. Design is generally a question of reasoning—perhaps from given premises—whereas expression is a question of instinct or emotion. But the design may obviously have logical beauty, and it might be held that such beauty is the only aesthetic quality that a metaphysical poem can have. In this connection

[1] *Cf.* Emile Mâle, *L'Art Religieux du XIIIe Siècle en France* (Paris, 1910, p. 1): "Le moyen âge a conçu l'art comme un enseignement. Tout ce qu'il était utile à l'homme de connaître, l'histoire du monde depuis sa création, les dogmes de la religion, les exemples des saints, la hiérarchie des vertus, la variété des sciences, des arts, et des métiers, lui était enseigné par les vitraux de l'église ou par les statues du porche."

it is valuable to note Dante's attitude as expressed in the dedicatory epistle to *Can Grande* (Epistola X of Mr. Paget Toynbee's edition of the Letters of Dante). In § 9 he describes the form or manner of treatment of the *Commedia* as " poëticus, fictivus, descriptivus, digressivus, transumptivus; et cum hoc definitivus, divisivus, probativus, improbativus, et exemplorum positivus ".[1] The conjunction of these several epithets shows either that Dante did not regard the " poetic " as incompatible with the definitive, the analytical, the probative, etc., or that otherwise he used the word *poeticus* in the sense we should use the word *lyric*, and did not see any reason why his poem should be wholly, or even mainly, lyrical. In § 15 of this epistle he states the aim of the whole and of the part as being " to remove those living in this life from a state of misery, and to bring them to a state of happiness "; and he goes on to say (§ 16) that " the branch of philosophy to which the work is subject, in the whole as in the part, is that of morals or ethics; inasmuch as the whole as well as the part was conceived, not for speculation, but with a practical object ". This emphasis on the doctrinal purpose of his poem, *totius et partis*, seems to prove very clearly, as the peculiar use of the word *poëticus* had indicated, that Dante did not regard his philosophy as inconsistent with his poetry, and this fact should be given its due weight, especially since there is a

[1] My quotations and translations are in each case taken from Mr. Toynbee's edition (Oxford, 1920).

tendency nowadays to regard the intellectual structure of the *Commedia* as irrelevant to its poetry. But nevertheless Dante nowhere presumes that his poem is poetical *because* it is philosophical, and the conclusion of the matter is, that while metaphysical poetry always exists in association with a mind that is didactic, insomuch as its life is a life of thought, yet it derives its poetic quality from another source, which is emotional. As an illustration we might represent thought and emotion as two separately revolving pulleys: one, emotion, has a revolution a thousand times greater than the other; but by the operation of a lever the two pulleys are connected, and immediately thought is accelerated to the speed or intensity of emotion.

In the case of Lucretius there is throughout a vigour and a resonance that are very attractive; in fact, the more his great poem is read the more it seems to cohere and become a unity, a part of one's mental life. And it is tempting to abandon all other pretensions and claim that this coherence of design and thought and unifying vitality is the sign and proof of the possibilities of metaphysical poetry. A sufficient case could be made out on this basis, but here I prefer to follow a more exact distinction, finding the nature of metaphysical poetry in the intensity rather than in the vigour of expression. For when the vitality of Lucretius's poem is analysed it is found to proceed from one of two causes: it is due either to the frequent interpolation of lyrical phrases, or, when these are absent, to a rather masterful rhetoric, a rather too facile manipulation of elemental metaphors. But he remains a very great poet, the most *interesting*, perhaps, of all the Latin poets. His lyric moods are very pure:

> nam saepe in colli tondentes pabula laeta
> lanigerae reptant pecudes quo quamque vocantes
> invitant herbae gemmantes rore recenti,
> et satiati agni ludunt blandeque coruscant;
> omnia quae nobis longe confusa videntur
> et velut in viridi candor consistere colli.[1]

The peculiar dichotomy of Lucretius's poem is seen when it is realized that lines so simply lyrical as these serve as a metaphor to explain the invisibility of atomic movement. Lyrics are embedded like jewels in the chain of an argument. The argument remains:

> inque dies quanto circum magis aetheris aestus
> et radii solis cogebant undique terram
> verberibus crebris extrema ad limina in artum,
> in medio ut propulsa suo condensa coiret,
> tam magis expressus salsus de corpore sudor

---

[1] II, 317-22. Munro's text (1864), who translates thus: "For often the woolly flocks as they crop the glad pastures on a hill, creep on whither the grass jewelled with fresh dew summons and invites each, and the lambs fed to the full gambol and playfully butt; all which objects appear to us from a distance to be blended together and to rest like a white spot on a green hill."

> augebat mare manando camposque natantis,
> et tanto magis illa foras elabsa volabant
> corpora multa vaporis et aeris altaque caeli
> densebant procul a terris fulgentia templa.[1]

Science was never so effectively written, before or since Lucretius's day. But though it is impossible to seize all the subtlety of lines written in a language we never speak, all the same I think it is evident that this beauty is a beauty of force; it is an aural clarion and deceives, and even deafens, the mind, whereas it should pervade it convincingly.

As the lyric lies like an episode breaking into the intellectual flow of *De Rerum Natura*, so in the case of the English metaphysical " school " we find an inverse process, giving rise to another possible misreading of the term " metaphysical poetry ": a metaphysical metaphor or concept is included in a poem predominantly lyrical in mood. In reality very few of the metaphysical school were metaphysical in any sense, and the name only adds confusion to literary criticism Their characteristics—" stranger than seven antiquaries' studies " —are well enough known; and their faults have

[1] V, 483-91. Munro translates thus: " And every day the more the heats of ether round and the rays of the sun on all sides compressed the earth into a close mass by oft-repeated blows on its outer edges, so that thus buffeted it was condensed and drawn together about its centre, ever the more did the salt sweat squeezed out of its body increase by its oozings the sea and floating fields, and ever the more did those many bodies of heat and air escape and fly abroad and condense far away from earth the high glittering quarters of heaven."

been ably summarized and controverted by Johnson in his *Life of Cowley*. But the quality that was really distinctive in the experiments of Donne and some of his followers Johnson missed altogether; all that he could grudgingly allow to " this race of authors " was a virtuous erudition: " To write on their plan it was at least necessary to read and think." In this way he did considerable injustice to Donne, as is shown by the quotations he uses, which never represent the Donne that appeals to a modern mind. In Donne we do as a matter of fact find the first consciousness of felt thought, and his compasses and mandrakes are small matters in comparison to this. The new consciousness is so incidental that at first it seems accidental; but it continues to be incidental, not only in the metaphysical school, but in others that came after them, and we must ascribe its rarity to its difficulty. It begins to be present in lines like the following:

> Earths hollownesses, which the worlds lungs are,
> Have no more wind than the upper valt of aire.
> We can nor lost friends, nor sought foes recover,
> But meteorlike, save that we move not, hover.
> Onely the Calenture together drawes
> Deare friends, which meet dead in great fishes jawes.[1]

It may be asked: what metaphysics is there in a passage like this? The only answer is that only a metaphysician could have written it. Only a mind habituated to thought would visualize its thoughts

[1] From *The Calme*, Oxford Edition, 1912, p. 178.

in precisely that way. Donne's metaphors, even when they are most "poetical", are still a part of his thought:

> All their proportion's lame, it sinkes, it swels.
> For of Meridians, and Parallels
> Man hath weav'd out a net, and this net throwne,
> Upon the Heavens, and now they are his owne.
> Loth to goe up the hill, or labour thus
> To go to heaven, we make heaven come to us.
> We spur, we reine the starres, and in their race
> They're diversely content t'obey our pace.
> But keepes the earth her round proportion still?
> Doth not a Tenarif, or higher Hill
> Rise so high like a Rocke, that one might thinke
> The floating Moone would shipwracke there, and sinke?[1]

Poorer poets bring lights into their rooms, but Donne, like all true metaphysical poets, strikes fire in the very process of his reasoning.

If we turn to a contemporary of Donne's—to George Chapman—we discover an even better augury of what the metaphysical poet might be. It would, in fact, be difficult to exaggerate the wealth of possibilities that came into existence with Chapman's individual poetry; but after Chapman came Milton, destroying this indigenous growth. Although a contemporary of Donne's, Chapman was not at the time often associated with Donne; he was not considered one of the metaphysical school—which shows, indeed, how prone contemporary opinion is to judge authors by their

[1] From *An Anatomie of the World: The First Anniversary*, Oxford Edition, pp. 239-40.

superficies: Donne by his conceits and Chapman by his "full and heightened style". When we get to the essence of these authors we find in Donne a mind poised at the exact turn of the course of philosophy—drawing his inspiration right back from scholastic sources, and yet at the same time eagerly surveying the new future promised by the science of Copernicus and Galileo. Chapman, on the other hand, is in a remarkable degree the forerunner of humanist philosophy—of Hume and Spinoza in particular. He is aware, above all things, of "the consent and sacred harmony of life". He brings ethics even into his title-page (e.g., *Caesar and Pompey*: A Roman Tragedy, declaring their Warres. Out of whose events is evicted this proposition: *Only a just man is a freeman*). And his theory of tragedy, as expressed in the dedication of *The Revenge of Bussy D'Ambois*, is more definitely didactic than Aristotle's even, and more uncompromising than Dante's theory of poetry: "And for the authentical truth of either person or action, who (worth the respecting) will expect it in a poem, whose subject is not truth, but things like truth? Poor envious souls they are that cavil at truth's want in these natural fictions; material instruction, elegant and sententious excitation to virtue, and deflection from her contrary, being the soul, limbs, and limits of an authentical tragedy." But who, in reading *The Revenge of Bussy D'Ambois*, pauses for an instant conscious of the boredom of its ethical purpose? It is, on the contrary, one of the most sustained poetic dramas in English literature. But the poetry is not "easy"[1]; it is musical, like lyrical poetry, but it has an opacity, or "charged" effect, characteristic of all good metaphysical poetry; as though behind each word lurked considerable processes of thought:

> And know ye all . . .
> That in this one thing all the discipline
> Of manners and of manhood is contained;
> A man to join himself with th' Universe
> In his main sway, and make (in all things fit)
> One with that All, and go on, round as it;
> Not plucking from the whole his wretched part,
> And into straits, or into nought revert,
> Wishing the complete Universe might be
> Subject to such a rag of it as he;
> But to consider great Necessity,
> All things as well refract as voluntary
> Reduceth to the prime celestial cause,
> Which he that yields to with a man's applause,
> And cheek by cheek goes, crossing it no breath,
> But, like God's image, follows to the death,
> That man is truly wise. . . .

The philosophical spirit in both Donne and Chapman was, I think, derived directly from Dante and the early Italian poets, rather than from more immediate forerunners in Spain and France; and it

[1] It is important, in this connection, to remember the dedicatory epistle to Ovid's *Banquet of Sense*, which embodies Chapman's very direct affirmations on the subject of his metaphysical poetry.

is to these, and particularly to Dante and Cavalcanti, that we turn for the most obvious illustration of the nature of metaphysical poetry. In reality there existed at that time a perfectly conscious theory of metaphysical poetry. It had come into existence with Guinicelli, who succeeded in escaping from the convention of direct lyricism, giving to his poetry a depth and beauty definitely related to a philosophical interest. "Amore e cor gentile" is not only one of the most beautiful love poems ever written: it is also one of the most metaphysical. Love is no longer an affair of the heart, but is rather an affair of the brain. It is a symbolism in which the most abstract ideals of the intellect can be made personal and actual. And it was this symbolism that became the sustaining element in all Dante's work. In the *Convivio* (Trattato Secondo, cap. i) Dante distinguishes the four values or interpretations of literature—the literal, the allegoric, the moral, and the anagogic. The first three are normal values and present no novelty. In the fourth value we have the whole meaning of metaphysical poetry. Dante defines the *senso anagogico* as occurring "quando spiritualmente si spone una scrittura, la quale, ancora nel senso litterale, eziando per le cose significate, significa delle superne cose dell'eternale gloria".[1] In effect, this value depends on a form of personification

[1] "When a writing is spiritually expounded, which even in the literal sense, by the very things it signifies, signifies higher matters of eternal glory."

which we have not developed to any extent in England (Donne's *Anatomy of the World* is the only example that occurs to me), and which consists of a bold interfusion of thought and actuality. The common idea of " personification " in literature is peculiarly bloodless: there is not, in fact, any idea at all of actually associating thought with a living person: personification is merely a convenience that enables us to address a virtue or an abstraction in the third person singular. It was far otherwise with Dante and Guido Cavalcanti: they in perfect seriousness identified their love of philosophy with their love of women; and in singing of their love of women they made an allegory that expressed their love of philosophy. In that manner they made their writings *sovra senso*, or anagogic. Or, more exactly, all experience, whether intellectual or sensual or instinctive, was regarded as equally and contemporaneously the subject-matter of their poetry. The result was a desirable continuity or coherence; imagination, contemplation, and sensibility becoming fused within the perfect limits of a human mind. " The poet was inspired with an overmastering desire to link the present with the past and with the future, to blend all knowledge into one coherent system, and to bring the experiences of life into one harmonious whole. For this purpose allegory was an indispensable instrument. But the basis of the allegory was no mere fancy. His conception of allegory postulates the existence of facts, for allegory is the agency by which earthly passion is brought into relation with Philosophy and Theology, and becomes their servant and interpreter."[1] In modern lyrical poetry this degree of coherence is never reached; we have instead a consciousness of the divorce of personality from the processes of thought. All the poet's senses and thoughts radiate from and return to one minute centre of self, and as a result he becomes disparate and insignificant in the process of nature, and a prey to *acedia* and despair. Thought, if indulged in at all, is not related to experience, though psychologically it may be a ratiocination balancing the abnormal exploits of the personality. But with Dante and Cavalcanti, and with Donne and Chapman, and even with Wordsworth, thought is the expression of experience—of all the experiences registered by the brain; and on the capacity of that brain for analysing its experiences, and even more on its capacity for selecting its experiences, will depend the value of the thought. If in addition that brain has the ability to reduce its thought to the emotional unit of the poem, we shall have the purest kind of metaphysical poetry as a result.

Dante achieved this result. The *Commedia* is the complete expression of a very complete mind—a mind that saw as much beauty in the *Summa* of St. Thomas Aquinas as in the episode of Paolo and Francesca, and did not find these beauties incon-

[1] William Walrond Jackson, D.D., "Introduction" to his translation of the *Convivio* (Oxford, 1909), p. 18.

sistent. It is in every sense a metaphysical poem, complete and unified, and as a whole is a perfect demonstration of the sufficiency of metaphysical inspiration. That the groundwork of the poem is metaphysical would not be disputed, but it is possible to show that the metaphysics is itself poetic, in detail as well as in design—that there exists at one and the same time abstract thought and feeling for that thought, expressed in poetry. I am not going to claim that this unity is to be discovered at all frequently in the *Commedia*. It is a difficult achievement, and in Dante's case there was even a special difficulty in that one of his " features " is the almost complete unoriginality of his thought: the world was not a problem to him, to be resolved by experimental effort, but the particularly neat scheme so amply provided by St. Thomas Aquinas. This vicariousness is not without its effect on the metaphysical quality of Dante's poetry, for the fusion of thought and emotion is surely more apt to be produced when thought has all the freshness of a personal discovery. But only *more* apt: that freshness is not exclusively the condition of emotion in thought is evident enough to all who enjoy an abstract argument. Besides, the exposition of a philosophy to which are attached no considerations of personal pride or vanity makes for the exclusion of all kinds of subjective impurities—makes, in fact, for that very objective clarity that is so distinctive of Dante's poem:

O abbondante grazia, ond'io presunsi
Ficcar lo viso per la luce eterna
Tanto, che la veduta vi consunsi!

Nel suo profondo vidi che s'interna,
Legato con amore in un volume,
Ciò che per l'universo si squaderna;

Sustanzia ed accidenti, e lor costume,
Quasi conflati insieme per tal modo,
Che ciò ch'io dico è un semplice lume.

La forma universal di questo nodo
Credo ch'io vidi, perchè più di largo,
Dicendo questo, mi sento ch'io godo.[1]

The history of Guido Cavalcanti's Canzone beginning "Donna mi priega" is the history of all metaphysical poetry. It is an analysis or definition of love, and was the most admired of Guido's poems in his own day. In the fourteenth century it inspired several elaborate commentaries, some of them by distinguished philosophers of the time. It passed into obscurity with the Renaissance; it probably had a brief revival of interest in the seventeenth and eighteenth centuries; but in the

[1] *Paradiso*, canto xxxiii, 82-93. Wicksteed translates as follows: "O grace abounding, wherein I presumed to fix my look on the eternal light so long that I consumed my sight thereon! Within its depths I saw ingathered, bound by love in one volume, the scattered leaves of all the universe; substance and accidents and their relations, as thought together fused, after such fashion that what I tell of is one simple flame. The universal form of this complex I think that I beheld, because more largely, as I say this, I feel that I rejoice."

nineteenth we find it the object of almost impassioned scorn. D. G. Rossetti describes it as " a poem beside the purpose of poetry, filled with metaphysical jargon, and perhaps the very worst of Guido's productions. Its having been written by a man whose life and works included so much that is impulsive and real is easily accounted for by scholastic pride in those early days of learning. I have not translated it, as being of little interest. . . ."[1] Even Gaspary cannot stomach it, and sarcastically remarks that the lady who had questioned Guido " must have been very learned if she was satisfied with his reply. . . . Here we have the apparatus of the scholastic philosophy, the logical divisions and distinctions, the definitions, syllogisms, and terminology of the schools. Image and sentiment, the foundations of all poetry, are entirely lacking ".[2] This latter sentence is entirely untrue, and I am indeed content to quote this famous poem as an example of true metaphysical poetry. The second stanza reads:

> In quella parte, dove sta memora,
> Prende suo stato, si formato, come
> Diafan dal lume, d'una oscuritate,
> La qual da Marte viene, e fa dimora.
> Egli e creato, ed ha sensato nome:
> D'alma costume, e di cor volontate:

---

[1] *The Early Italian Poets*, Introduction to Part II.

[2] *The History of Early Italian Literature*, by Adolph Gaspary, translated by Hermann Oelsner (1901), pp. 207-8.

Vien da veduta forma, che s'intende,
Che prende nel possibile intelletto,
Come in suggetto, loco e dimoranza.
In quella parte mai non ha possanza,
Perche da qualitate non discende.
Risplende in se perpetuale effetto:
Non ha diletto, ma consideranza;
Si che non puote la gir simiglianza.[1]

One might leave the subject there, counting on the sufficiency of Cavalcanti and Dante, and of Donne and Chapman; but there are certain " obvious " poets that one can't neglect to mention if only to disclaim them—I mean particularly Milton, Shelley, and Browning. Wordsworth is different. But Milton, in his later phase, perhaps did more to destroy the true tradition of metaphysical poetry than any other agent. His thought

[1] It is difficult to translate such concentrated poetry as this. Charles Lyell (*The Lyrical Poems of Dante Alighieri*, London, 1845) has made the following attempt (p. 134):

Within the soul's recess where memory dwells
Love has its seat, there formed as brightness is
By light, in thing transparent that was dark;
Which darkness is from Mars, and permanent.
Love is produced, and has its name from sense;
A habit of the soul, a will of the heart;
It springs from beauty seen and contemplated;
Which takes, in the receptive intellect,
A dwelling-place, as in a subject fit.
There, matter it has none, nor has it weight;
For purely spiritual is its quality.
Love shines transplendent, long as beauty charms.
In contemplation is its whole delight,
Hence it can yield no likeness to itself.

was a system apart from his poetic feeling, and in the violence wrought by his too forceful fashion he almost crushed the life out of an only too subtle advance of human consciousness. He did not think poetically, but merely expounded thought in verse: psychologically he was conscious all the time of a dualism—on the one side the thought to be expounded, on the other side the poetic mould into which his thought had to be smelted. The true metaphysical poet is conscious of no such dualism: his thought is in its very process poetical. This distinction so briefly expressed may seem a trifle upon which to dismiss so established a reputation as Milton's is in this particular sphere, and it must be admitted that the whole matter needs careful analysis and consideration; for the present I prefer not to endanger a good cause by enlisting a doubtful ally. Shelley, too, I prefer to leave unquoted: his sentiments were too vague to bring him within the scientific definition of philosophy underlying the assumptions of this essay; and when he meant to be metaphysical he was merely mystical. As for Browning, he was neither mystical nor metaphysical, and I am not sure that it would not be legitimate to say that he was just wordy. It may be admitted, however, that he has very definite claims to be considered as a psychological poet; and if "Bishop Blougram's Apology" is not so good of its kind as is Cavalcanti's canzone beginning "L'ardente fiamma della fiera pesta" (it is not so sincere), yet "Bishop Blougram" and parts of *The Ring and the Book* and certain of the *Parleyings* are good enough to establish the *genre* in its own rights. But the *genre* is definitely psychological, consisting of the analysis of motives and personalities, and differing entirely from the metaphysical, which should confine itself to the statement of ideas. Leibniz has defined an intelligent author as one who includes the most of reality in the least possible compass,[1] and it would be difficult to improve on this definition. And in that case it is difficult to see how psychological poetry, which is descriptive, can compete with metaphysical poetry, which is synthetic. It is for this reason, if for no other, that Wordsworth tends to emerge out of the immediate welter of his epoch with something more of solidity than we can associate with the merely descriptive evocations of his contemporaries. In fact, I might go a long way to find a better example of metaphysical poetry than certain lines from the fragment of *The Recluse*:

> . . . I must tread on shadowy ground, must sink
> Deep—and, aloft ascending, breathe in worlds
> To which the heaven of heavens is but a veil.
> All strength—all terror, single or in bands,
> That ever was put forth in personal form;
> Jehovah—with his thunder, and the choir
> Of shouting Angels, and the empyreal thrones—
> I pass them unalarmed. Not Chaos, not
> The darkest pit of lowest Erebus,
> Nor aught of blinder vacancy, scooped out

---

[1] *Discourse on Metaphysics*, § v.

By help of dreams, can breed such fear and awe
As fall upon us when we look
Into our Minds, into the Mind of Man,
My haunt, and the main region of my song.
. . . .
. . . if I oft
Must turn elsewhere—to travel near the tribes
And fellowships of man, and see ill sights
Of madding passion, mutually inflamed:
Must hear Humanity, in fields and groves
Pipe solitary anguish; or must hang
Brooding over the fierce confederate storm
Of sorrow, barricadoed evermore
Within the walls of Cities; may these sounds
Have their authentic comment,—that even these
Hearing, I be not downcast or forlorn!

The first part of this quotation is a gesture, and it may be advanced that as such it comes dangerously near to being rhetorical. But rhetoric is only reprehensible when it is hollow, as it mostly is; when it is compact with thought, as this rhetoric of Wordsworth's is, it is powerful beyond any other mode of expression. Blake recoiled in horror from three of these lines: he saw in them a rebellion against the very basis of humanistic religion. And if to-day we can no longer share Blake's apprehension, we can instead appreciate the profundity, the intellectual significance, and the emotional power of these verses. The second part of the quotation does not lack something of such qualities also, but I use it rather with the special intention of illustrating how words like "confederate" and "authentic comment" can be lifted from their prosaic origins and made the very keywords of a poetic vigour.

With Wordsworth the metaphysical tradition in English poetry for the time being ends. The possibility of recovering this lost tradition remains to be considered.

I began by defining metaphysical poetry as the emotional apprehension of thought, and I am not sure that I can do better than leave the definition simply so, trusting that the quotations I have meanwhile made use of may quite sufficiently illustrate my meaning. It has been seen very noticeably, I hope, that a degree of economy is implied in the word " apprehension "—that economy of thought, in fact, breeds its corresponding intensity, which is to be identified with the poetry itself. More anxiously I hope that it has been seen in exactly what sense the epithet " emotional " has been used. Now that my illustrative matter is complete, as far as may reasonably be allowed, " emotional apprehension " should appear as a fairly " hard," even as a necessarily " dry ", process. It is important beyond everything, in this era of emotional or " commonsense " philosophies, not to confuse this mental process in which emotion is the product of thought, with that other vaguer, easier process, which is the emotionalization of thought, or thought as the product of emotion. Metaphysical poetry is determined logically: its emotion is a joy that comes with the triumph of the reason, and is not a simple instinctive ecstasy. It is, finally, but the precise statement of such abstractions as the poet derives from his experience. Perhaps, in the scholastic sense, it is the poetry of universals.

As for an ideal of present service, I would gladly refer the reader to Mr. Santayana's formulation of it in *Three Philosophical Poets*—a work of grace and fervour to which this essay must stand as a brief and halting appendix. I would not have ventured even upon this appendix but for a point of departure I wish to make. " Throw open " (Mr. Santayana concludes) " to the young poet the infinity of nature; let him feel the precariousness of life, the variety of purposes, civilizations, and religions even upon this little planet: let him trace the triumphs and follies of art and philosophy, and their perpetual resurrections—like that of the downcast Faust. . . ." There is a Latin generosity about this formulation, a certain expansiveness that does not seem to accord with our present ideas. Infinity is a dangerous word, in art no less than in philosophy, and we should do well to avoid it—or give it a definite meaning. But to define an ideal in any exact way is very difficult. For what, after all, is the material of poetry, and particularly of metaphysical poetry, but just vaguely " life "—*i.e.*, the poet's life, the compound of all his experiences? But from another point of view we can see that the poet is in a very real sense the product of his age—witness especially Dante. It is perhaps worth while, then, to refer to the characteristics of our own age, and in that way arrive at some more definite idea of the possibilities of metaphysical poetry to-day. This leads us on to very opinionative ground; we strike deeply into subconscious prejudices. But, generally, we can recognize the disintegration of religion, and even of more secular crowd-emotions like patriotism, and with this disintegration the disappearance of some of the most powerful sources of poetic inspiration. To what degree this disintegration is permanent is another question, and not one to be discussed here. At the worst we may trust that the crowd, as an organized society, will find an equivalent outlet for its emotional forces; and it does not yet seem necessary to admit the extreme pessimism of so much recent German speculation on this subject. And for our immediate concern we may even claim a certain independence for the poet. If he is the product of his age, yet he is not generated by the pressure of a specific unanimism, but rather stands within his environment and absorbs the spectacle around him; and in this sense negation is as good a sounding-board for thought as any more positive state of society. And however pitiful our social life may be, yet there does exist an intelligent minority of considerable vigour and positive achievement: I refer particularly to the modern physicists, whose work would seem to provide a whole system of thought and imagery ready for fertilization in the mind of the poet. For, if the assumptions of this essay are accepted, it will be seen that science and poetry have but one ideal, which is the satisfaction of the reason. Aesthetic satisfaction is not, as is too often assumed, the satisfaction of the senses (the senses are never satisfied), but *is* the satisfaction of the co-ordinating judgment of the intellect—in symmetry, in rhythm, and in all the properties of universal truth. For science we accept without question the axiom that logical method and the satisfaction of reason are the final tests to be used in the attainment of a system of truth, but for art such an ideal appears at first sight to be paradoxical and detrimental—even as science, in another age, found the ideals of religion inimical, and nearly fatal. Ideals, however, survive only so long as they serve the interests, economic or emotional, of the multitudes among which they exist: they, as all human attempts at fixation, are at the mercy of more brutal forces. Very few ideals —perhaps only those immuring the instincts of self-preservation—are so old as history; and such an ideal as scientific method in poetry must be accepted subject to the contingency of all ideals. The scientific ideal does at any rate carry us into the full stream of all that is valuable in our age. Science has established a large number of " phenomena ", but these phenomena remain discreet. They lack harmonic unity. Perhaps mathematical philosophy is working in one direction to establish this unity; metaphysical poetry, working in a different direction, can, without presumption, aim to the same end.

III

PURE POETRY

DEFINITIONS of poetry are extremely rare; it is not a subject about which many people have felt it necessary or desirable to be dogmatic. The critics have been content with descriptive classifications, the true poets with their practice, and the plain man with his enjoyment. Therefore, we should honour Mr. George Moore's *Anthology of Pure Poetry* with a criticism more pertinacious than the casual reviews that appeared at the time of its publication. For Mr. Moore is an imaginative artist who should possess a direct intelligence of art, and is, moreover, at least by pretension, an objective artist from whom we might expect a detached and logical statement of his views. There is no doubt that his Anthology is a work of criticism; it is one of the few that have such a rational justification. And Mr. Moore has done his work well: the Anthology is consistent with its avowed aim and makes a very formidable pretence of infallibility. It is, what Mr. Moore intended it to be, " a real advancement in the study of poetry ".

Pure poetry, Mr. Moore holds, is born of admiration of " the only permanent world, the world of things.[1] Ideals, thoughts, reflections, become common quickly; an idea is mine to-day, yours to-morrow, and the day after to-morrow it is on the barrel-organs. Every ten years morality, patriotism, duty, and religion take on meanings different from those they wore before, and that is why each generation, dissatisfied with the literature that preceded it, is inspired to write another literature round the new morality, the new patriotism, the new duty, the new religion, a literature which seems to the writers more permanent than the literature their fathers wrote, but which is destined to pass away as silently."

Now Mr. Moore has just a little way above this passage quoted Gautier's sonnet, " La Tulipe ", in evident security that *its* beauty has not passed away. I wish to avoid the arrogance of a younger generation, but I must confess that in my street I find this sonnet on the barrel-organs. If I wanted to be violent I should say that it is insipid, lifeless, of dead perfection. It is not instinct with any energy, whether of the mind or the senses. Its imagery is stale, and ever was commonplace, *e.g.*, " plus cher qu'un diamant ". The heraldic metaphor in the second stanza is inappropriate, and would be disdained by a poet not possessing the

[1] It is curious to note that in modern French criticism the same phrase (" la poésie pure ") has quite a different, and even an opposite, meaning. It is objective enough in its mode, but for its material (as, for example, in the poetry of Paul Valéry) it resorts to the world of abstraction.

particular affectations of Gautier's period. The last image is worst of all: " mon calice fait comme un vase de Chine." The metaphor is not vague to anyone with a knowledge of the history of taste; " un vase de Chine " conjures to the mind some demoded K'ang Hsi prettiness of the kind affected by the brothers de Goncourt, by Whistler, and by Gautier himself. The history of taste shows that things, equally with ideas, thoughts, and reflections become common quickly; have their day of fashion and pass, to lie embedded in the wordy music of " objective " poets.

But this is not the whole of the question. The word " objective " has its definite uses, but I was surprised to find Mr. Moore using so psychological a term. It does, as a matter of fact, lead us into the very heart of the question. Mr. Moore has other phrases, such as " innocency of vision " and " a vision almost detached from the personality of the poet ", which save him from a too rigid adherence to the cant phrases of scientific discussion. I am not anxious to revert to that more arid plane, but, once a psychological term is made an excuse for a poetic dogma, I see no alternative to the exploration of other equally psychological possibilities; nor can we altogether avoid metaphysical terms, for Mr. Moore implies them. What, for example, does he mean by " pure " poetry, if not poetry which attains *absolute* beauty, for it is beauty, we are told, not subject to change. " Time cannot wither nor custom stale poetry unsicklied o'er with the pale cast of thought." Mr. Moore is not alone in his wish to stem " the desolating tide of subjectivity ", nor in wishing to see a more impersonal conception of art. But what does he mean by his terms. I have never thought of Mr. Moore as particularly classical in his attitude towards life or in his art; he writes, it is true, possibly the best intimate style of his generation. For the rest he is as romantic and as subjective as anyone possibly could be. He is a typical Rousseauist, exploiting his sensations for the benefit (or to the detriment?) of his art. He never rises above these sensations, to transmute them into universal terms. He is for this reason incapable of any of the major forms of art, and has had to confine himself to the romantic exercises of a novelist and raconteur. He may pride himself that *Esther Waters*, for example, is a tolerably objective performance, but it may be doubted whether it is more than a pastiche in the manner of Flaubert. It has no inner conviction of necessity, like *Madame Bovary*, no intelligent significance, like *L'Education Sentimentale*. It is difficult, in fact, to know what Mr. Moore means by objectivity. He seems to imagine that the objective faculty is solely concerned with " things ", and by " things " he means the material objects of everyday life. And presumably subjectivity is correspondingly only concerned with images or ideas. But subjectivity is rather an attitude that when completely developed includes the whole of the sensible universe. It is the total orientation of an individual's sensibilities, and all things in his mind, whether thoughts or things, are set in one direction. Equally objectivity involves all aspects of experience, and an idea can be as impersonal to its beholder as any material thing. It is only to be remembered that the completely objective man, equally with the completely subjective man, is a fiction of our milder mythologies.

When we turn to the actual examples of objectivity in English poetry selected by Mr. Moore, we begin to doubt the applicability of the term at all. Commenting on " La Tulipe ", Mr. Moore has observed that the fatal phrase " fait comme un vase de Chine " is a signature. And if this phrase is a signature, what of " While greasy Joan doth keel the pot ", " Within her lawnie continent ", " He show'd me lilies for my hair ", " And like a dying lady, lean and pale ", " The skies they were ashen and sober "? What are these and a thousand other lines but personal signatures, evident to the most casual reader? What is there " objective " about accents that strike as freshly and as intimately as a friend's voice? A passage from Newman's essay on Literature may be considered in this connection. " Literature ", he writes, " is the personal use or exercise of language. . . . Language itself in its very origination would seem to be traceable to individuals. Their peculiarities have given it its character. We are often able, in fact, to trace particular phrases or idioms to individuals; we know the history of their rise. Slang surely, as it is called, comes of, and breathes of the personal. The connection between the force of words in particular languages and the habits and sentiments of the nations speaking them has often been pointed out. And, while the many use language as they find it, the man of genius uses it indeed, but subjects it withal to his own purposes and moulds it according to his own peculiarities. The throng and succession of ideas, thoughts, feelings, imaginations, aspirations, which pass within him, the abstractions, the juxtapositions, the comparisons, the discriminations, the conceptions, which are so original in him, his views of external things, his judgments upon life, manners, and history, the exercise of his wit, of his humour, of his depth, of his sagacity, all these innumerable and incessant creations, the very pulsation and throbbing of his intellect, does he image forth, to all does he give utterance, in a corresponding language, which is as multiform as this inward mental action itself and analogous to it, the faithful expression of his intense personality, attending on his own inward world of thought as its very shadow: so that we might as well say that one man's shadow is another's as that the style of a really gifted mind can belong to any but himself. It follows him about *as* a shadow. His thought and feeling are personal, and so his language is personal."[1]

Mr. Moore would, of course, agree with

[1] *The Idea of a University*. Edition of 1919, pp. 275-6.

Newman's eloquent and decisive affirmation. He knows perfectly well that the most distinctive feature of all the poems he has selected is not their objectivity, not their approach to a "pure" or absolute type of beauty, but just this personal seal, this integrity of style and thought, of thought and character. If Mr. Moore had wanted to use a psychological phrase, he might with more exactness have resorted to terms which would rasp as uncouth neologisms on his ear—I mean the terms *extraversion* and *introversion*. For these imply not, like objectivity and subjectivity, the mind and a state or existence external to it, but merely conditions of the mind itself.

But he might then have discovered that for his purpose there was no need to press the distinction. For personalities may be extravert or introvert, and are both by turns and together; and in this respect poets—true poets, poets such as Mr. Moore has honoured in his Anthology—are no different from the rest of us. The real distinction lies elsewhere.

It lies foremost in this accent of personality which Newman analyses. And if the personality were not a composite of moods, there would be no more to it than that. But we can distinguish further.

Expression in poetry may arise, I think, from three different states of mind. It may be the skilled expression of a preconceived idea; it may be the witty expression of an inspired idea; or it may be the impulsive expression of an emotion.

Landor's " Hamadryad " is of the first type, Herrick's " To gather flowers Sappha went " of the second, Blake's " Introduction to Songs of Innocence " of the third. In this way we could classify the whole of Mr. Moore's Anthology. But this is not a classification that provides us with any criterion. What then *is* your criterion? Mr. Moore might ask. The answer is: the quality of intelligence inherent in the poem. But what is intelligence? might be the further query. It is a question I have tried to answer generally in this book; here it will be sufficient to say that it is the same faculty of " direct apprehension " already distinguished by mediaeval philosophy, and since then somewhat compromised, in differing degrees, by Descartes, Spinoza, and Bergson. It is dangerous perhaps to describe it as a " faculty ", for it is in reality but one aspect of the single faculty of apprehension. It is perhaps only the distinction between reason which is concentrated on a single object and reason which is discursive. It is a distinction clearly and for all time made by no less an authority than St. Thomas Aquinas: " intelligere enim est simpliciter veritatem intelligibilem apprehendere: ratiocinari autem est procedere de uno intellecto ad aliud, ad veritatem intelligibilem cognoscendam. . . ."[1]

[1] St. Thomas, *Sum. theol.*, i, q. lxxix, 8. Quoted by J. Maritain, *Antimoderne* (Paris, 1922), p. 32.

IV

THE FUTURE OF POETRY

PROFESSOR SAINTSBURY, improving on Hazlitt, once defined poetry as "the vivid and consummate expression, in metre, of an impression furnished by object, event, passion, imagination, fancy, or whatsoever humanity can be, do, suffer, or experience". This is more inclusive than Hazlitt's phrasing, but also more pedantic: the words "in metre" have taken the place of what is, in Hazlitt, good psychological observation; for Hazlitt makes the vividness of the impression excite "an *involuntary* movement of imagination and passion", and produce "by sympathy a certain modulation of the voice or sounds expressing it". Professor Saintsbury has in effect obscured those very modern notions of the unconscious and the involuntary reflex which Hazlitt had so presciently divined. But both definitions agree in the universal scope they give to the poetic mind: nothing, absolutely nothing, is immaterial or irrelevant. That being so—the sphere of poetry being co-extensive with all our most intimate and daily interests—how does it come about that poetry to-day has, in the words of

Mr. Trevelyan,[1] " ceased to be a great popular and social art ".

There are two obvious possibilities: either the poets wilfully ignore the natural subject-matter of their art, which is to say that they turn away from the immediate aspects of life; or, alternatively, they fail to give those aspects " vivid and consummate expression ". But these obvious possibilities involve a third possibility, which is much more fundamental: that the form of poetry is such that it fails to absorb its natural subject-matter, and for that reason is ignored by those who feel the need for a direct and impulsive mode of expression. Any discussion, therefore, of the future of poetry itself, must take, first of all, this rather arid procedure of examining the possibilities of poetic technique. Even that wider supposition now current, that the functions of poetry have been largely replaced by the functions of science—which is to say that the imagination now expresses itself in a material more precise than imagery—even this question cannot arise until we have admittedly exhausted all the possibilities of poetic technique. For what *is* poetry that it should be discarded as an outworn instrument? They who discard it must first define it. In fact, they must do more: they must defy all possible definitions and revolutions that the art adopts under the pressure of this siege.

Mr. Trevelyan has written a very depressing

[1] *Thamyris, or Is there a Future for Poetry?* by R. C. Trevelyan. London, 1925.

pamphlet, for all his hopes are half-hearted, and all his reforms at the mercy of an uneasy pedantry. His suggestions for the enlivening of poetic technique amount to no more than the research for subtleties of quantity in blank verse and " all sorts of new possibilities of lyrical structure ". He seems to be aware of the inadequacy of the remedy for the disease: hence his despair. His pamphlet appears in a series devoted to prophecies; but having no real confidence in the future of poetry, Mr. Trevelyan confines himself to generous ineptitudes.

He can only suggest two main influences at work in every fertile and creative age of literature: naturalism (" an awakened sensitiveness to the suggestive beauty of the outside world ") and antiquarianism (" the fascination exercised by the masterpieces of earlier periods and alien cultures "). He has perhaps never conceived the possibility of both these concepts being irrelevant to the consciousness of an age—for irrelevant they have been in the past (in Ancient Chinese and Teutonic art, for example) and irrelevant they may be in the future. This lack of prophetic enterprise on Mr. Trevelyan's part is perhaps related to his conception of the general functions of poetry. " The main function of verse," he writes, " is deliberately, by its structure to regularize rhythm, and so to create emotion artificially." This seems to be opposite to the psychological truth; for surely the first function of verse is to express emotion, and only secondarily, and quite carelessly, to create a corresponding emotion in the reader. Mr. Trevelyan's "deliberately" contradicts Hazlitt's "involuntarily", but it is Hazlitt who is the better psychologist. The "controls" in poetry operate in quite a different way, being confined to the selection of the significant among our emotions, and to their organization into some objective structure. The intelligence uses the emotions as the motive power of intellectual concepts, but it does not, and indeed cannot, deliberately create them.

This perhaps brings us nearer to the cause of the unpopularity of modern poetry. But it is not so much the unpopularity of poetry as its priority that matters. Poets can afford to be unpopular because it is the price they pay for being in advance of the general sensibility. At all great epochs of change and of crystallization it is the medium of verse that has hitherto embodied the first and the final accents of intelligence. The first formulation of the particular spirit of the Renaissance is found in the poetry of Jacopone; and it was only under the direct influence of Franciscan literature that the plastic arts took on, in Giovanni Pisano and Giotto, the elements of a new conception of life. The priority of poetry seems to hold good for all epochs of western civilization down to and including the Romantic Movement of the last century. It holds good even of later and minor movements, such as that of the Symbolists in France and of the Pre-Raphaelites in England. But of the definitely new conceptions which promise to be distinctive of the twentieth century we find little sign in poetry; and in this sense Mr. Trevelyan's despair is justified. There is, that is to say, no adequate literary equivalent in England for the impressive organization and intellectual content of the modern movement in painting. There may be psychological reasons for this unusual precedence of the visual arts, and to speculations of this kind it is tempting to devote some space. But for the present we must consider the practical possibility of inherent defects in traditional poetic form. Why that form did not succumb to the forces that changed design in the plastic arts is still another question. It is largely a question of a lack of intelligence at certain crises in the history of poetry since Baudelaire.

Such a crisis is always marked by a discussion of the technique of verse, and no such discussion has been so general and on the whole so profound as the one that marked the emergence of the classical English style in the Elizabethan period. And in this discussion there were no documents so practical and so decisive as Thomas Campion's *Observations in the Art of English Poesie* (1602) and Samuel Daniel's *A Defence of Ryme* (1603).[1] Sidney's more famous *Apologie for Poetrie*, published in 1595, had been written about 1581, before the dawn. It has a more general and pervasive charm than these two militant pamphlets, because it is

[1] The Bodley Head Quartos, No. XIV. London, 1925.

written from a more absolute standpoint. At the same time it lacks the empirical interest of the later works, which were composed at the highest and intensest moment in the history of the English tongue. Here we touch the pulse of a crisis, feel the life flowing, and see intelligence determining the result. The cause in question was more than the ostensible one—the use of rhyme. It was the cause of native and original vigour against academic and pedantic bonds. Surprisingly it is Campion, inveighing against " the childish titillation of riming ", who furthers the academic cause. In the setting out of his case he makes certain just observations on the abuse of rhyme, as " that it inforceth a man oftentimes to abjure his matter, and extend a short conceit beyond all bounds of arte ", and his experiments in unrhymed verse are lively and were not without their influence on the development of blank verse. He brought even Daniel to an admittance that " a tragedie would indeede best comporte with a blank verse, and dispence with Ryme ", and to an advocacy of certain precautionary measures against " this overglutting the eare with that alwayes certaine, and ful incounter of Ryme ". But Campion could advance no very positive reasons for the abjuration of all rhyme beyond the fact that the custom of the Greeks and Latins was against it. His graceful pamphlet was easy prey to Daniel, who is full of lusty good sense and the right humour of originality. He goes straight to the point, and contends that the genius of our language has its own peculiar laws:

"Every language hath her proper number or measure fitted to use and delight, which, Custome intertaining by the allowance of the Eare, doth indenize, and make naturall. All verse is but a frame of wordes confinde within certaine measure; differing from the ordinarie speach, and introduced, the better to expresse mens conceipts, both for delight and memorie. Which frame of wordes consisting of *Rithmus* or *Metrum*, Number or Measure, are disposed into divers fashions, according to the humour of the Composer and the set of the time; And these *Rhythmi* as *Aristotle* saith are familiar amongst all Nations, and *è naturali & sponte fusa compositione* : And they fall as naturally already in our language as ever Art can make them; being such as the Eare of it selfe doth marshall in their proper roomes, and they of themselves will not willingly be put out of their ranke; and that in such a verse as best comportes with the Nature of our language."

There are two observations in this passage which are of present moment, for they possibly indicate considerations which we have since forgotten. One relates to what we might call the inherent rhythm of our language, determined by custom and evident to the ear, and the other to the disposition of number or measure according to *the set of the time*. It is possible that by "the set of the time" Daniel meant no more than the dictates of fashion; but even this phrase may have a useful sense, implying the instinctive harmony of expression and actuality. And here we come to the crux of the modern situation; for have we any assurance that modern poetry has arrived at this intimate sympathy with the pace or rhythm of contemporary life which is the condition of all vigorous art? But there are two questions here which must not be confused: the nature of poetic rhythm, and its relation to what we must call the rhythm of life. " Every versifier ", Daniel observes in another place, " that well observes his worke, findes in our language . . . what numbers best fitte the Nature of her Idiome, and the proper places destined to such accents, as she will not let in, to any other roomes then into those for which they were borne." " A dunce like myself ", said Swinburne, " measures verse by ear, not by finger." This latter remark is quoted by Professor Sonnenschein, whose concise treatise[1] is devoted to a new conception of rhythm which has the merit of " fitting the facts " in a remarkably inclusive way. One thing in the eternal discussion of rhythm is certain, that verse, both historically and creatively, takes its form as a rhythmical sequence independent of any analysis into feet and measures. First the poet and then the metrist. Professor Sonnenschein

[1] *What is Rhythm?* An essay by E. A. Sonnenschein. Accompanied by an appendix on Experimental Syllable-Measurement, in which Stephen Jones and Eileen Macleod have co-operated. Oxford, 1925.

keeps this truth well in mind, and his definition of rhythm is based on it. " Rhythm ", he says, " is that property of a sequence of events in time which produces on the mind of the observer the impression of proportion between the durations of the several events or groups of events of which the sequence is composed." Among the merits of this definition is the fact that it speaks of *durations*; " for *time*, in the sense of the duration of events, is the fundamental feature of rhythm ". It also speaks of *events* in time, and implies the possibility of measuring them. And thereby hangs a story. For Professor Sonnenschein, or rather his assistants in the Phonetics Laboratory at University College, London, make use of a wonderful instrument called the kymograph, which by its operations promises to put at rest all the age-long controversies of the metrists. For the kymograph, like the camera, cannot lie.

Briefly, the kymograph can measure exactly the duration of every syllable in speech; it can therefore reveal the exact quantity of spoken verse. For example, a simple line of Tennyson's, when measured, shows the following ratios of duration:

The long light shakes across the lakes
12 : 31 : 27 : 45 : 7 : 34 : 9 : 55

When this scientific measurement is applied on a large scale to the main body of " refined English verse ", the results show beyond doubt that " quantity is nothing less than a *structural element* in the best kind of English verse, side by side with accent". Syllables are only relatively long or short, and even then may vary with the context; or they may be of equal value in a foot (isosyllabic), or protracted, or even, where the rhythm demands it, merely imaginary. Professor Sonnenschein is, of course, mainly concerned with the analysis of traditional verse forms, and no one interested in this aspect of the subject can afford to neglect his book. He does not, however, make any attempt to apply his definitions and discoveries to the extension of the possibilities of poetry. He does not seem to realize, for example, that his definition of rhythm is not merely applicable to refined extracts from Tennyson and Keats, but that it is equally applicable to "The Strayed Reveller" and "The Waste Land". In fact, Professor Sonnenschein's definition, without more ado, substitutes the element of proportion in rhythm for the element of regularity; and this is precisely what the best *vers libriste* poets, in France, England, and America, have been contending for. One cannot deny proportion to a rhythm like this, which is contemporary free verse:[1]

sunlight was over
our mouths fears hearts lungs arms hopes feet hands
under us the unspeaking Mediterranean bluer
than we had imagined

---

[1] From a poem by E. E. Cummings, in "1924", no. 2, August 1924.

a few cries drifting through
high air
a sail a fishing boat somebody an invisible spectator
maybe certain nobodies laughing faintly
playing moving far below us
perhaps one villa caught like pieces
of a kite in the trees here
and here reflecting
sunlight.

nor to this passage, from " The Strayed Reveller ":

Is it then evening
So soon ? I see, the night-dews,
Cluster'd in thick beads, dim
The agate brooch-stones
On thy white shoulder;
The cool night-wind, too,
Blows through the portico,
Stirs thy hair, Goddess,
Waves thy white robe!

Nor can one, for that matter, concede regularity to a rhythm like this:

Pray, do not mock me:
I am a very foolish, fond old man,
Fourscore and upward, not an hour more nor less;
And, to deal plainly,
I fear I am not in my perfect mind.
Methinks I should know you and know this man;
Yet I am doubtful: for I am mainly ignorant
What place this is, and all the skill I have
Remembers not these garments; nor I know not
Where I did lodge last night.

and lines like these, which demand such an

elaborate quantitative analysis, are in effect totally free from any but the most superficial regularity:

> Open, ye everlasting Gates, they sung,
> Open, ye Heav'ns, your living dores; let in
> The great Creator from his work returnd
> Magnificent, his Six days work, a World;
> Open, and henceforth oft; for God will deigne
> To visit oft the dwellings of just Men
> Delighted, and with frequent intercourse
> Thither will send his winged Messengers
> On errands of supernal Grace. So sung
> The glorious Train ascending: He through Heav'n,
> That open'd wide her blazing Portals, led
> To Gods Eternal house direct the way.

If, then, we are to substitute for the concepts of measure (that is, for regular, accented feet) a concept of rhythm dependent on nothing but its own innate rightness as tested by the ear, we must inquire more closely into the nature and origins of such rhythms. How are they come by? The conventional metrist will say that at any rate in the case of Shakespeare and Milton, and even in the case of Arnold, they are variations on the basis of a regular measure. But this is casuistry, for all rhythm, even the rhythm of prose and of speech, is only perceptible by contrast to an hypothetical norm of regularity—a uniform temporal beat or simple iambic sequence. Certainly all free verse of rhythmical structure is related to such a norm or basis. But actually no rhythms are consciously constructed by a system of normal measurements: they are rather spontaneous sense perceptions.

And any comparative study of rhythms reveals the fact that they are relative. They vary from age to age and from language to language. Chinese and Polynesian rhythms are perceptible to us, but they are foreign to our habits. English rhythms have a good deal in common with Germanic rhythms, but both are quite different from French or Spanish rhythms. Even within the limits of our own language, if we observe carefully purely local dictions, we find surprisingly different rhythms. A man from Newcastle and a man from Hull speak in entirely different *tempi*. But we must beware of a loose connotation of the word "rhythm", which is better kept for aesthetic effects. We can, however, resort to the word "idiom", so aptly used by Daniel. A living language analyses into idioms: idioms are the live organisms of speech—words are molecules and letters atoms. Now this organic unit, this idiom, is instinct with rhythm; it has irrefrangible intonation, and poetic rhythm is but the extension and the aggregation of these primary rhythms. Even measured, regularly accented verse is successful only in so far as it makes use of or accommodates itself to these idioms. Free verse, which includes the slightest as well as the widest divergence from regular pattern, is but the free use of these idioms.

Idioms arise out of the contacts of daily life. They are the response of the human organism to the elements around it. They reflect the speed of life, the pressure of life, its very essence. Idioms are the vocal chimings-in of man in the rhythm of life, and have their parallels in the beating of drums and the dancing of limbs. All the arts are built up from these primary elements, and their reality, their actuality, depends on this strict relation. To build up poetry with dead idioms is like living a life of dead habits and obsolete manners. But such is precisely the sickness of nearly all modern poetry: it rings false in the actual turmoil of the day.

We can only seize the real rhythm instinctively. It *has* been found—in the modern ballet, in American rag-time music, and in a minute quantity of modern poetry. But when we have found the rhythm we are only at the beginning of art. We have found no more than the instruments of art.

"It is not the observing of *Trochaicques* nor their *Iambicques* [writes Daniel in one place] that wil make our writings ought the wiser: All their Poesie, all their Philosophie is nothing, unless we bring the discerning light of conceipt with us to apply it to use. It is not bookes, but onely that great booke of the world, and the all-overspreading grace of heaven that makes men truly judiciall."

That warning against pedantry applies equally to the makers of new rhythms, for no amount of originality will benefit us if it lack "the discerning light". Technique we may learn from observations, but this final necessity is a gift of a more individual nature, depending not so much upon the influences of environment as upon an inborn capacity. Or, to speak more exactly, it depends upon a convergence of these two factors—upon the right mind co-operating with the widest experience, and then freely expressing itself.

V

PSYCHO-ANALYSIS AND CRITICISM

Any attempt to raise literary criticism above the vague level of emotional appreciation through the incorporation of scientific elements is sure to meet with opposition, not only from the great majority of critics, who depend on their emotions, but also from more serious people who imagine that the prescribed boundaries of decent critical activity are being broken down. To the former set we can only present our weapons; with the latter we must reason, and our task is all the more difficult for the lack, in England, of any scientific tradition. Our critics have, as a rule, resorted to nothing more distant from their subject than common-sense. Perhaps the only successful attempt of a more ranging kind was that of Coleridge, who did consciously strive to give literary criticism the rank of a mental science by relating it to what he called " the technical process of philosophy ". Unfortunately, what this technical process amounted to in Coleridge's day was a very innate kind of metaphysical speculation, speculation rather dim across an interval of more than a hundred years. We have become more empirical, and the general effect of the growth of science has been to discredit transcendental reasoning altogether.[1] Traditional criticism, therefore, in so far as it can claim to be fundamental, is a structure whose very foundations have perished, and if we are to save it from becoming the province of emotional dictators, we must hasten to relate it to those systems of knowledge which have to a great extent replaced transcendental philosophy. Physics, demanding as it does such impressive modifications of aspect and attitude, provides the most general background for all subsidiary efforts, but for the literary critic psychology gains an intimate importance because it is so directly concerned with the material origins of art.

The critic, in approaching psychology, will not be altogether disinterested: he will merely raid it in the interests of what he conceives to be another science, literary criticism. This science—if it is permissible to call it a science—really covers a very wide field indeed. It is the valuation, by some standard, of the worth of literature. You may say that the standard is always a very definitely aesthetic one, but I find it impossible to define aesthetics without bringing in questions of value which are, when you have seen all their implications, social or ethical in nature. There is no danger, therefore (or very little danger), in the direction of a too inclusive conception of the critic's

[1] I imply " in the general mind ". That empirical science can ever dispense with all aprioristic processes is a vulgar error to which the general tenour of this book is opposed.

function: danger, and death, is rather to be found in the narrow drift of technical research, the analysis of the *means* of expression and so on. But it is a proper complaint against literary criticism in general that it has reached no agreed definition of its boundaries, and until it does it has no serious claim to be considered as a science. It is only because I want to distinguish one kind of literary criticism from another, even as you distinguish astronomy from astrology, or chemistry from alchemy, that I resort to a pretence of science. That distinction established, there is no need to carry the pretence any further: it is not necessary, I mean, to simulate the vocabularies of science.

Another consideration meets us at the outset of this inquiry, and the more one realizes it the more it appears to put the whole utility of our discussion in doubt. I mean the very obvious difference in the subject-matter of our two sciences: psychology is concerned with the processes of mental activity, literary criticism with the product. The psychologist only analyses the product to arrive at the process: art is, from this point of view, as significant as any other expression of mentality. But of no more significance: its significance does not correspond to its value as literature. The psychologist is indifferent to literary values (too often, alas, even in his own work), and may even definitely deplore them, especially when they represent the trimming of subjective phantasies under the influence of some objective standard or tradition. But in any case the psychologist has found and will always find a large body of material in the imaginative literature of all epochs: that side of the question is so obvious that I shall pay no more attention to it. But whether in the nature of things it is possible for such psychology to add anything positive to the principles of literary criticism is more in doubt. Analysis involves the reduction of the symbol to its origins, and once the symbol is in this way dissolved, it is of no aesthetic significance: art is art as symbol, not as sign. Alfred Adler, whom I have found, for my purpose, one of the most suggestive of the psycho-analytical school, has recognized this, pointing out that "*the attraction of a work of art arises from its synthesis*, and that the analysis of science profanes and destroys this synthesis".[1] This is perhaps *too* respectful an attitude; there is no need to make a mystery of art. But it is an easy and an unprofitable task to translate into crude terms of sexual phantasy a poem like William Blake's "I saw a Chapel all of Gold". One might as well confess that the impossibility of avoiding such a translation is a serious defect in the psychological critic; for him the naïve acceptance of such a poem is impossible; here at least there is no beauty without mystery. Luckily for the critic, few poets are so artless as Blake, and meaning and intelligence tend to be remote in the degree that they are profound.[2]

[1] *Individual Psychology*, English edition, 1924, p. 268.

[2] When this remoteness occurs, as in the case of Shakespeare's *Hamlet*, then I think it inevitably follows that any

I have perhaps laid sufficient emphasis on the general limitations of the psychological method in criticism. Before I begin with my main task, which is to explore the uses of psycho-analysis to literary criticism, let me deal with one of its misuses. It perhaps concerns literature rather than criticism, but we must all realize by now that no good artist exists who is not, at every point of his career, firstly a good critic. The work of art emerges within a radiation of critical perceptions. But, criticism apart, the author who imagines that he can start from psycho-analysis and arrive at art is making a complete mistake. No literature, not even a novel, can arise out of a schematic understanding of the phenomena of life. Art has only one origin—experience. Art is itself a schematic construction; an order imposed on the chaos of life. As such it has its own delicate and individual laws. But to conceive art as the illustration of science, or even as the embodiment in tangible fiction of aprioristic views of the universe, is surely a final sort of degradation, a use of the imagination more finally discredited than any it is possible to think of.

explanation that psychology can offer for the complicated strands of poetic creation tends to quicken our general sensibility. Reasoning and mechanism do not lose their value because we follow step by step the process of their operation; and I think a poetic process is exactly analogous. It is where you have, not a dynamic process, but a static symbol, that analysis is without any critical significance, and may be positively destructive of the aesthetic effect. I shall return to this point in dealing with Dr. Ernest Jones's study of *Hamlet.*

That is not to say that the study of psycho-analysis is entirely without object for the would-be novelist or poet. It might at least help him to realize, more quickly and more reasonably than the normal man would realize from his own experience, such facts as the subjectivity of love,[1] and the general law of determinism in which all our emotions and ideals are bound. Again, the novelist cannot in his plot ignore with impunity what we might now call the psycho-analytical probabilities. Then surely, it might be said, the examination of such probabilities is an opportunity for the critic well versed in psycho-analysis. But it does not follow. Here, admittedly, is the opportunity of the psycho-analyst, straying from his strict domain, eager to show what fools these artists be. But the literary critic will ignore this obvious use of psycho-analysis, if only for the sufficient reason that to a critic of any worth these psychological defects in a work of the imagination will appear as literary defects. You cannot write well—you cannot, as we say, " create " your atmosphere—without a " germ of the real ". Any psychological unreality will, in the end, be apparent in some insincerity of style or method.

In the endeavour to discover the critical utility of psycho-analysis I will, merely for dialectical reasons, formulate three questions.

[1] *Cf.* Jacques Rivière, "Notes on a Possible Generalisation of the Theories of Freud" (*The Criterion*, vol. i, no. iv, pp. 344-5).

I. What general function does psycho-analysis give to literature?

II. How does psycho-analysis explain the process of poetic creation or inspiration?

III. Does psycho-analysis cause us to extend in any way the functions of criticism?

I ask the first question, apart from its intrinsic interest, to make sure from both points of view—that of psycho-analysis and that of criticism—that we have the same subject-matter in mind. I ask the second question—again apart from its intrinsic interest—to make sure that we have a common conception of what " creative " literature is. We can then, without fear of misconstruction, deal with the third question—which is the question I have all the time been leading up to.

To most questions in psycho-analysis there are three answers—those respectively of Freud, Jung, and Adler—and as a mere expropriator in this territory I take the liberty to lift my material from whichever quarter suits me best. Perhaps in this matter of the general function of literature Jung is the only one of the three to work out a theory in any detail. Freud and Adler do not seem to press the question beyond its individual aspect, to which I shall come in my second question. Jung's theory springs from that general principle of contrasted attitudes which is really the characteristic method of his psychology—the contrasted attitudes which he calls introversion and extraversion, a fundamental division of the self which may be traced in every activity and which we may variously paraphrase as the opposition between subject and object, between thought and feeling, between idea and thing. Now Jung's theory is that living reality is never the exclusive product of one or the other of these contrasted attitudes, but only of a specific vital activity which unites them, bridges the gulf between them, giving intensity to sense-perception and effective force to the idea. This specific activity he calls *phantasy*, and he describes it as a perpetually creative act. " It is the creative activity whence issue the solutions to all unanswerable questions; it is the mother of all possibilities, in which, too, the inner and the outer worlds, like all psychological antitheses, are joined in living union."[1] Jung further differentiates *active* and *passive* phantasy—the latter a morbid state which we need not stop to consider here. Active phantasy he describes as owing its existence " to the propensity of the conscious attitude for taking up the indications or fragments of relatively lightly-toned unconscious associations, and developing them into complete plasticity by association with parallel elements ".[2] Now although Jung remarks that this active phantasy is " the principal attribute of the artistic mentality " he nowhere seems to have pressed home the conclusions which are surely latent in his theory, namely, that the poetic function is nothing else

[1] *Psychological Types*, English edition. London, 1923, p. 69.
[2] *Ibid.*, p. 574.

but this active phantasy in its more-than-individual aspect. The poet, in fact, is one who is capable of creating phantasies of more than individual use—phantasies, as we should say, of universal appeal. Thus art has for psycho-analysis the general function of resolving into one uniform flow of life all that springs from the inner well of primordial images and instinctive feelings, and all that springs from the outer mechanism of actuality—doing this, not only for the artist himself, from whose own need the phantasy is born, but also, by suggestion and by symbol, for all who come to participate in his imaginative work.

And here at last the processes of psycho-analysis and literary criticism run together. "Whether the actual social validity of the symbol", says Jung, "is more general or more restricted depends upon the quality or vital capacity of the creative individuality. The more abnormal the individual, *i.e.*, the less his general fitness for life, the more limited will be the common social value of the symbols he produces, although their value may be absolute for the individuality in question."[1] Now "the social validity of the symbol" is a phrase which I confess I would willingly annex for literary criticism, for it is to some such concept that any thorough critical activity leads us, and though I think the "symbol" in literature (we should never call it that) is something more precise, more deliberate, something more intelligent than

[1] *Op. cit.*, p. 380.

the normal unconscious symbol of psychology, yet, if psycho-analysis can help us to test its social validity, then it can in this respect be of some use to literary criticism.

I come to the individual aspect: do we gain any further light from the psycho-analysis of the creative mind? How does the modern psychologist define inspiration, and does his definition bear any correspondence to our critical concepts? It is the general problem of the psychology of genius and far too big a field to explore in any detail here. But it will, I think, be worth while to examine one or two relevant aspects of the question. I think that in the mind of every artist (though I think particularly of the literary artist) there are two contrary tendencies. In one direction he is impelled to shuffle off conscious control and to sink back into his primitive mind, where he knows he can find a fresh elemental imagery, a rich though incoherent phantasy. It is the disjointed fortuitous world of dreams—day-dreams. In the other direction he is impelled to establish strong affective tendencies—ideals of moral beauty, of plastic form, of order and architecture. These resolve themselves into some kind of unity and form the goal towards which, consciously or unconsciously, the artist's life is formed. You get the harmony of perfect art when the two forces achieve a balance. I think this is all a matter of psychological observation, but it has a direct bearing on what we may call the central problem of literary criticism—I mean the question of romanticism and classicism. There is, therefore, a peculiar echo of reality in these words of André Gide, written from a purely literary standpoint, in reply to an inquiry on Classicism:

" It is important to remember that the struggle between classicism and romanticism also exists inside each mind. And it is from this very struggle that the work is born; the classic work of art relates the triumph of order and measure over an inner romanticism. And the wilder the riot to be tamed the more beautiful your work will be. If the thing is orderly in its inception, the work will be cold and without interest."[1]

It is this riot within that we ordinarily call inspiration, and a good deal of attention has been devoted to its description by modern psychologists. By some it is assumed to be a function of the unconscious mind, which is credited with autonomous activity, with powers of incubation and elaboration. Most people will be familiar with Poincaré's account of his own experiences in mathematical discovery (*Science et méthode*, chap. iii), where he

[1] " Il importe de considérer que la lutte entre classicisme et romantisme existe aussi bien à l'intérieur de chaque esprit. Et c'est de cette lutte même que doit naître l'œuvre ; l'œuvre d'art classique raconte le triomphe de l'ordre et de la mesure sur le romantisme intérieur. L'œuvre est d'autant plus belle que la chose soumise était d'abord plus révoltée. Si la matière est soumise par avance, l'œuvre est froide et sans intérêt."—Réponse à une enquête de la Renaissance sur le classicisme, 8 Janvier 1921 (*Morceaux Choisis*, p. 453).

describes how some sudden illumination would come to him after a period during which conscious application to the problem had been abandoned. Poincaré attributed these sudden illuminations to the unconscious workings of the mind, but he did not really advance any proof of his hypothesis, and I do not think the idea is any longer entertained by psychologists. Modern psychologists explain sudden illumination or inspiration rather as due solely to a fortuitous entry into activity of ideas which are immediately associated and seized upon in their happy combination,[1] and this theory is, I think, entirely satisfactory as an explanation of poetic inspiration. It will not, perhaps, satisfy the poets themselves, who all, like Blake, imagine that they take down from the dictation of angels. But we are none of us very exact in the description of our own emotional states. What really happens may perhaps be described in the following way: you have in the first place the prevailing affectivity, the latent ideal of form or thought; what forms this ideal, what brings it into being, I shall explain in a moment. You have, next, the bringing into activity fortuitously of some image or memory which until the moment of inspiration had lain latent in the unconscious mind; this fortuitous image is as it were criticized by the excited interest; it is selected or rejected; and if selected it is developed and transformed by the ever prevalent

[1] *Cf.* E. Rignano, *The Psychology of Reasoning.* London, 1923, p. 129.

affectivity. If the affective tendency is suddenly and strongly roused, then you get a state of emotion, bringing with it an intensity of awareness to all the images and ideas that follow in the wake of the first fortuitous image. This is the state of ecstasy. Images seem to leap from their hiding-places all fully equipped for the service of the ideal or affective tendency. But even in this state of animation or ecstasy I believe that a good deal of selection and rejection of images still goes on. However, normally a creative act occurs when the exact word or image is found. And the full creative process is but a summation of many of these primary creative moments.

If this be a correct description of the process of poetic creation—and it is based both on my reading of psychology and on the analysis of my own putative experiences—then the part that may be played by suggestion or self-hypnosis in the encouragement of such states is obviously considerable, and I think that in time a complete technique of inspiration may be evolved. That this will result in a vast increase in the number of poets need not be feared, for nothing ever comes out of the unconscious mind that has not previously been consciously elaborated or sensibly felt: the product of the unconscious mind will always strictly correspond with the quality of the conscious mind, and dull intellects will find as ever that there is no short cut to genius.

It will be observed that there is nothing essential

or peculiar in this description of the creative process: it is just what occurs in any man's mind when he is suddenly endowed with a " bright idea " Where then must we seek for an explanation of the abnormality of the artist? Obviously, I think, in the nature of the ideal or affective tendency to which his whole creative life is subservient. And for an explanation of this I return to the psycho-analysts.

Freud and his disciples would trace back the formation of the abnormal mentality of the artist to the period of infancy. " Analysis of this aspiration " (for ideal beauty), says Dr. Ernest Jones, " reveals that the chief source of its stimuli is not so much a primary impulse as a reaction, a rebellion against the coarser and more repellent aspects of material existence, one which psychogenetically arises from the reaction of the young child against its original excremental interests."[1] The repression of such tabooed interests may indeed contribute to the details of aesthetic activity, but this particular hypothesis seems far too limited in conception, and far too poorly supported by facts to account for the variety and profundity of aesthetic expression in general. The less specialized theory of Adler seems to offer a clearer explanation. According to the principles of " individual psychology ", " every neurosis can be understood as an attempt to free oneself from a feeling of inferiority in order

[1] *Essays in Applied Psycho-Analysis*, 1923, p. 262.

to gain a feeling of superiority"[1] The feeling of inferiority usually arises in the family circle, and the compensatory feeling of superiority is usually a phantasy so absurd in its high-set goal of godlikeness that it remains in the unconscious; it is repressed by the communal standards of logic, sympathy, and co-operation. This buried sense of superiority is present in most of us, but the artist takes the goal of godlikeness seriously and is compelled to flee from real life and compromise to seek a life within life;[2] and he is an artist in virtue of the form and ideal perfection which he can give to this inner life. The neurotic fails to create a formal phantasy, and lapses into some degree of chaos. Now it is worth observing, as a confirmation of the general truth of this theory, that the most general period for the formation of the superiority-complex coincides with the most general period for the outburst of the poetic impulse. I mean the time of the awakening of the adolescent sexual instincts, the time of the withdrawal of parental protection, the period of intense conflict between instinctive desires and social control. I think there can be no doubt that the artist is born of this conflict. Freud himself lends support to this view. He says: The artist " is one who is urged on by instinctive needs which are too clamorous; he longs to attain to honour, power,

[1] Alfred Adler, *The Practice and Theory of Individual Psychology*, English edition. London, 1924, p. 23.
[2] *Cf.* Adler, *op. cit.*, p. 8.

riches, fame, and the love of woman; but he lacks the means of achieving these gratifications. So, like any other with an unsatisfied longing, he turns away from reality, and transfers all his interest, and all his libido too, on to the creation of his wishes in the life of phantasy." And Freud goes on to explain how the artist can, by the expression and elaboration of his phantasies, give them the impersonality and universality of art and make them communicable and desirable to others—"and then he has won—through his phantasy—what before he could only win in phantasy: honour, power, and the love of woman".[1]

The essential point to notice is that psycho-analysis seems to show that the artist is initially by tendency a neurotic, but that in becoming an artist he as it were escapes the ultimate fate of his tendency and through art finds his way back to reality. I think it will be seen now where psycho-analysis can be of some assistance to the critic—namely, in the verification of the reality of the sublimation of any given neurotic tendency. The psycho-analyst should be able to divide sharply for us, in any given artistic or pseudo-artistic expression, the real and the neurotic. There is much in literature that is on the border-line of reality: it would be useful for the critic to be able to determine by some scientific process the exact course of this border-line. But again I would suggest that in all

[1] Sigm. Freud, *Introductory Lectures on Psycho-Analysis*, English edition. London, 1922, pp. 314-5.

probability the critic could determine this borderline by general critical principles; but psycho-analysis might be a shorter path to the test; and in any case it would supply collateral evidence of a very satisfactory kind. Psycho-analysis finds in art a system of symbols, representing a hidden reality, and by analysis it can testify to the purposive genuineness of the symbols; it can also testify to the faithfulness, the richness, and the range of the mind behind the symbol.

There still remains the third question that I propounded: Does psycho-analysis modify in any way our conception of the critic's function? The clear difference in subject-matter, already defined, makes it unlikely that we shall find any fundamental influence. It is merely a question of what kind of attitude, among the many possible to the critic within the strict limits of his function, psycho-analysis will stress. It does not, so far as I can see, amount to anything very definite—anything more precise than a general admonition to tolerance. Human activities are shown to be so inter-related, so productive of unrealized compensations, that any narrowly confined application of energy and intelligence results in a distortion of reality. Hence the futility of a purely categorical criticism—which may be illustrated by reference to "the Hamlet problem". During the past two hundred years an extensive body of criticism has accumulated around Shakespeare's cryptic masterpiece. The difficulty, for the critics, is to account within the canons of art for Hamlet's hesitancy in seeking to revenge his father's murder. Dr. Ernest Jones has given a fairly complete summary,[1] which I will summarize still further, of all the various theories advanced at different times. There are two main points of view: one, that of Goethe and Coleridge, finds a sufficient explanation of the inconsistencies of the play in the temperament of Hamlet, whom they regard as a noble nature, but one incapable of decisive action of any kind—" without that energy of the soul which constitutes the hero ", as Goethe expresses it. The second point of view sees a sufficient explanation in the difficulty of the task that Hamlet is called upon to perform. Both these theories have been decisively refuted, time and time again, from the very facts of the play, and finally criticism has manœuvred itself into a paradoxical position, boldly asserting that the tragedy is in its essence " inexplicable, incoherent, and incongruous ". This is the position taken up with so much force by Mr. J. M. Robertson. " Robertson's thesis " (I quote from Dr. Jones's summary) " is that Shakespeare, finding in the old play ' an action that to his time discounting sense was one of unexplained delay, elaborated that aspect of the hero as he did every other ', ' finally missing artistic consistency simply because consistency was absolutely excluded by the

[1] *Essays in Applied Psycho-Analysis*, 1923, pp. 1-98, "The Problem of Hamlet".

material '; he concludes that Hamlet is ' not finally an intelligible drama as it stands,' that ' the play cannot be explained from within ' and that ' no jugglery can do away with the fact that the construction is incoherent, and the hero perforce an enigma, the snare of idolatrous criticism '. " All this can be said, and said intelligently, and with a convincing absence of emotional prejudice. But it leaves us curiously dissatisfied. We cannot dismiss so easily the personal intensity of expression throughout the play, and such intensity, such *consistent* intensity, gives the play a unity which the old academic criticism has failed to perceive. It seems that here is a case of an instrument not large enough, or not exact enough, to measure the material in hand.

And where literary criticism fails to account for its problem, what can psycho-analysis do? Dr. Jones has shown that it will claim to do a great deal, and he has elaborated in his study of Hamlet a psychological explanation of the peculiar problems of the play. He sees in Hamlet's vacillation the workings of a typical " complex "—the Œdipus complex, as it is called by the psycho-analysts. That is to say, the mental peculiarities of Hamlet, expressed throughout the play with such vividness and actuality, can be explained as the consequences of " repressed " infantile incestuous wishes, stirred into activity by the death of the father and the appearance of a rival, Claudius. With the use of this hypothesis Dr. Jones can explain, and explain very plausibly, all the difficulties and incoherences of the action; and he finds in the play such an exact delineation and such a rich wealth of detail that he cannot but conclude that in writing *Hamlet* Shakespeare was giving expression to a conflict passing through his own mind. There is a certain amount of biographical confirmation of this further hypothesis in the circumstances of the composition of the play, but not facts enough, alas, to be of much use to any solution of the problem.

It would be interesting to follow this application of psycho-analysis to literary criticism into further detail, but perhaps I have indicated enough of Dr. Jones's theory and method to show the possibilities of this new approach to the problems of literature. Whether Dr. Jones's explanation is tenable or not, it does provide what is at present the only way out of a critical impasse, and for that reason alone it merits serious consideration. At the very least it points to a defect in our critical methods, for the failure of literary criticism to deal with *Hamlet* is largely due to its approach to the problem along too narrow a front: we must always be prepared for literature refusing to fit into our critical categories. Criticism is a process of crystallization, of the discovery and elaboration of general concepts; but we must be prepared for the voyage of discovery leading us into strange and unfamiliar tracts of the human mind.

That is one way in which psycho-analysis

supplies a corrective to the narrowness of criticism. I find still another, tending to the same end. I have referred before to the eternal opposition of the classic and the romantic: to this blind difference under the influence of which even the best of critics race into untenable dogmatisms. Can psycho-analysis resolve this difficult conflict and supply us with a common standpoint?

I think it can—particularly the psycho-analysis associated with the name of Jung. Jung has devoted his best work to the analysis of psychological types. As I have mentioned before, he distinguishes between two fundamental types, the extraverted and the introverted, determined according to whether the general mental energy of the individual is directed outwards to the visible, actual world, or inward to the world of thought and imagery. These two fundamental types are further subdivided into types determined by the functions of thinking, feeling, sensation, and intuition, but the psychological types so determined do not form hard-and-fast categories into which the whole of humanity can be classified: they are merely indications of extensive divisions which merge one into another. But in our particular sphere they do supply a scientific basis for the description of literary types. You will find, for example, that the romantic artist always expresses some function of the extraverted attitude, whilst the classic artist always expresses some function of the introverted attitude. Now this suggests that the critic, like the psychologist, should take up a position above the conflict, and although his own psychological state may lead him to sympathize with one school or the other, yet as a scientific critic he must no longer be content with a dog-in-the-manger attitude. Again, he must broaden the basis of his criticism: he must see the romantic and classic elements in literature as the natural expression of a biological opposition in human nature. It is not sufficient to treat the matter one way or the other as a question of intellectual fallacy; it is a question, for the individual, of natural necessity; and criticism must finally, for its general basis, resort to some criterion above the individual.

I would like to indicate, in conclusion, what I think might be a fruitful direction for further work in the application of psycho-analysis to literature. Recent theories explain memory, and indeed most of the characteristics of mind, on a basis of physiological " traces " left by experience. Experience may be individual or collective, and what happens individually must also happen collectively, and those instincts and experiences incidental to the struggle for adaptation and existence leave their traces on the mind when, and in so far as, it functions collectively. The accretion of innumerable traces ensures a set response to environment. A given physical structure of the brain results in certain inevitable forms of thought, and these Jung, following Burckhardt, calls primordial images. Such images eventually crystallize as myths and religions,[1] and psychology has already devoted a good deal of attention to the relation of such myths and religions to the unconscious processes of which they are the expression. Sometimes these collective ideas or primordial images find expression in literature, which, from an evolutionary point of view, has been regarded as a rational mythology.[2] Jung quotes from a letter of Burckhardt's these very suggestive sentences:

" What you are destined to find in *Faust*, that you will find by intuition. *Faust* is nothing else than pure and legitimate myth, a great primitive conception, so to speak, in which everyone can divine in his own way his own nature and destiny. Allow me to make a comparison: What would the ancient Greeks have said had a commentator interposed himself between them and the Œdipus legend? There was a chord of the Œdipus legend in every Greek which longed to be touched directly

[1] This process, however, should not be held to exclude the possibility of the specific origin of myths. The opposition recently created between psycho-analysts and ethnologists of the Manchester school is largely fictitious. The origin of the myth may be a plain event devoid of psychological significance : the elaboration of this event into a mythical structure, often over a period of many years, even centuries, may all the same be a process for which we should seek an explanation in psychology.

[2] *Cf.* Th. Ribot, *Essai sur l'Imagination Créatrice*, Paris, 1900, p. 114: " La Littérature est une mythologie déchue et rationalisée."

and respond in its own way. And thus it is with the German nation and *Faust*."[1]

This train of thought, allied to what we know of the possibilities of psycho-analysis in dealing with myths, seems to suggest the further possibility of relating the types actualized by the poetic imagination to their origin in the root-images of the community. In this way criticism would possess still another basic reality on which it could ground the imaginative hypotheses of art. Whether criticism, under the guidance of psycho-analysis, could go still further and indicate the needs of the collective mind, is perhaps too venturesome a suggestion to make. But with the advance of reason we have lost the main historic content of the collective mind: the symbols of religion are no longer effective because they are no longer unconscious. We still, however, retain structural features of the mind that cry for definite satisfaction. The modern world is uneasy because it is the expression of an unappeased hunger. We need some unanimity to focus the vague desires that exist in the collective mind. Will the psychologist unite with the critic to define and to solve this problem?

[1] C. G. Jung, *Psychology of the Unconscious*, English edition, 1918, p. 490.

VI

THE DISCIPLES OF DIDEROT

Bless me, sir, a terrible progeny! they belong to the tribe of *Incubi.*—The Rev. Dr. Folliott, in *Crotchet Castle.*

We may safely leave aside any general enquiry into the dramatic theories of Diderot: they make on the whole rather a wearisome display of dialectic, only redeemed by Diderot's loquacious instinct: the father of the encyclopaedias, even in his most encyclopaedic moments, managed to vivify his prose with the accents of his tongue—which, if we are to believe his contemporaries, was by far the best witness to his real powers. But on one question of dramatic art Diderot remains a very authentic voice; and the voice is the voice of a prophet. The lesser theologians who derive from his original gospel still thrive with that luxuriance so characteristic of later theologies of every kind. For this reason it seems worth while to isolate the particular theory to which I refer: to see the shape it took in the mind of Diderot; to follow its reverberations in the larger critical intelligence of Lessing; to connect it with the conditions that gave it birth; and finally to ask whether the theory has any general validity to-day and why it should continue to be imposed as a dogma and an inhibition to genius.

Diderot had a romantic dislike for anything approaching a systematic exposition of his ideas. "O faiseurs de règles générales, que vous ne connoissez guère l'art, et que vous avez peu de ce génie qui a produit les modèles sur lequel vous avez établi ces règles, qu'il est le maître d'enfreindre quand il lui plaît!" So he exclaims midway in his own rambling essay *De la Poésie Dramatique*, and we know the insufferable systems he had in mind. But Diderot carried his formlessness to the verge of obscurity: we get lost in the maze of his irrelevancies and divagations and turn with relief to some such summary abstract as that made by Emile Faguet in his *Dix-huitième Siècle*. We cannot, however, in that way dispense with Diderot. The essential Diderot is precisely in those divagations which, having little to do with the matter in hand, carry, however, a sudden illumination into the mind. As when he writes: "Les plans se forment d'après l'imagination; les discours, d'après la nature." Or as when he draws this distinction between satire and comedy: "La satire est d'un tartuffe, et la comédie est du Tartuffe. La satire poursuit un vice. S'il n'y avait eu qu'une ou deux Précieuses ridicules, on en aurait pu faire une satire, mais non pas une comédie." The whole of the *Paradoxe sur le Comédien* is packed with observations on the art of acting—some of them derived directly from Garrick—which modern actors might still study with advantage. And this essay is the more interesting because its particular theme, namely, that the actor plays best, even in scenes of great passion or emotion, when still retaining his self-possession, is in direct contradiction to the general tenor of Diderot's naturalism.

Three main ideas emerge from the voluble chaos. One we may dismiss as no longer alive—the contention that the dramatist should interest himself in the *conditions* rather than the *characters* of his creations; that is, in the attributes of fatherhood, rather than in the personality of a father It was one of those futile attempts, always doomed to failure because they are directed from some standpoint of external theory, to limit the subject-matter of art. Diderot's second idea—that the theatre should act as a moral agent—we may dismiss for other reasons. Diderot held this idea very strongly, as, indeed, did most of his contemporaries, including Voltaire. It was imagined, I think, that the direct contact between the living agents of the drama (the actors) and the audience was of an immediacy unknown in any other forms of art, and man being so much impelled by imitative instincts, here, in the theatre, was the ideal field for the inculcation of the virtues. I doubt if one could find a modern critic (so sensitive have they become) to defend a theory so bald in its utilitarian motives; but if we have by now shelved this problem, it is not so much that we have got rid of it by solving it, or that we have dismissed it as insoluble. It is rather that we have given it a different incidence. We have subjectivized it. We no longer expect (or even condone) the direct moral purpose in art, but, if we have any critical principles of adequate reach, we demand a quality in the mind of the artist which works out, in the end, as the moral equivalent of this purpose. That is to say, the work of art no longer expresses a moral purpose: it implies one. This is perhaps a subtle distinction, but it is of the essence of the modern critical position.

Diderot's third plea, and his most insistent one, was for a more natural mode in the theatre. As M. Faguet has remarked, what is natural in one age is conventional in the next—"and this is necessary, since, only to maintain the same degree of convention, one must react against the conventional every fifty years." For Diderot, naturalism implied many things—all of them at that time of a revolutionary nature. He would abolish the stilted alexandrine of the traditional drama and substitute the natural prose of speech; he would do away with the tedious formality of the *discourse* in drama, and introduce instead the quick action and animated gestures of normal life; and then, in a large manner, he pleaded for the *genre sérieux* in comedy, and for the domestic theme in general.

It is not part of my intention to trace the origin of these ideas (they mostly came from England) or to examine the causes, mainly social, which determined them. It is more to my purpose to observe that the general procedure so cynically foreshadowed by M. Faguet does not in this case seem to have been followed. It is now about one hundred and seventy years since these theories were enunciated and we still have critics who write as though these things had been in the essence of drama for ever, and as though Elizabethan tragedy, and much else before and after not conforming to the naturalistic standard, had been but a regrettable aberration from some inevitable norm. But before discussing the modern situation I would like to glance at the immediate reception accorded to Diderot's naturalistic theories by the clear intelligence of Lessing.

§ 2

The *Hamburg Dramaturgy* is the modern *Poetics* —at least, since Aristotle there is no work devoted to the theory of the drama so illuminating and suggestive as this series of occasional criticisms given to the world between 1767 and 1769. The whole burden of the work is: Back to Aristotle! —and Lessing does not hesitate to acknowledge that he considers the *Poetics* as infallible as the *Elements* of Euclid (in a Euclidean world!). The French, on the other hand, he conceived as having misapprehended the rules of ancient drama: from Corneille and Racine to Voltaire they had built up a structure on misinterpretations and mistranslations of the text of Aristotle, and on a perverse emphasis of his incidental illustrations, regardless of the general logic of the argument. The state of the drama which Diderot, with his empirical sense, conceived as unnatural, Lessing conceived as false learning, false logic, false history. From this point of view Diderot, too, must be brought up against the infallible principles of Aristotle and reproved for the excess of his reactions. The fresh sight that animated Diderot's mind came from England—from English philosophy with its realistic bent and from English plays with their life despite the rules: and this same inrush of reality was operative in Lessing's mind and in Germany very generally at that time. But Lessing kept his head. We must not, he said, confound all rules with bad rules, or count all discipline as pedantry. There was a real danger, he felt, of wantonly throwing away the experience of all past times and demanding from the poet that he should discover his art anew.

§ 3

Diderot, in the course of his distinction between character and conditions, had been drawn into a facile generalization to the effect that whilst the characters of a tragedy must be in some degree particular, those of a comedy are always general. "The comic genus has species, the tragic has individuals. The hero of a tragedy is such and such a man; he is Regulus or Brutus or Cato, and no other. The prominent persons in a comedy, on the other hand, must represent a large number of mankind." This assertion of Diderot's aroused all Lessing's vigour and he had little difficulty in showing that not only is there no justification for such a dogma in the *Poetics*, but also that such a doctrine would be contrary to the very principles of art. It is *art*, of course, in a very classical sense, but precisely there is the difference between these two minds. Diderot's plea is a plea for the personal equation in art: it is the plea of an incipient romantic.

Lessing, however, frankly admits that Aristotle does not altogether solve the problem. There are two senses of generality: in the first sense a general character means a character in which what has been observed in one or more individuals is welded together; and Lessing calls this type an *overladen* (überladen) character. "It is more the personified idea of a character than a characterised person."[1] In the other sense a general character means a character in which an average or mean proportion has been abstracted from many or all individuals —that is, a *common* (gewöhnlicher) character. Aristotle's καθόλου is obviously generality in this second sense. It seems to have been left to Ben Jonson to elaborate the first conception—the embodiment of abstract character.

The possibility of two such conceptions leaves

[1] The quotations from the *Hamburgische Dramaturgie* are given in Helen Zimmern's translation (London, 1879), but I have taken the liberty of making one or two very slight amendments.

Lessing in a state of doubt and indecision. Is there a real distinction? Can the same character illustrate both the overladen and the common abstraction, and what is the value of the *individual* after all? Lessing left the problem unsolved; and it may appear remote enough at this day—a distinction not worth reviving, belonging to the dead logomachy of dramatic theory. But there are two things to bear in mind: firstly, that if we are to emerge from our present confusion in drama, we must return to distinctions of which perhaps this is one. Secondly, if we can now *solve* the problem, it will make a difference to its importance. It may be that in modern psychology, especially as it relates to the classification of types, we shall find a solution of the problem that baffled Lessing. "What then?" the modern dramatist will be tempted to ask. "Assuming that your psychological criticism does establish a single generality—what then? I create personalities and little do I care for your *types*, so long as my creations *live*." It would only show how difficult it is to get the modern dramatist (or the modern dramatic critic) even to consent to the terms of classical art. It would be quite hopeless to expect him to draw a distinction between *his* function, as he so largely formulates it, and the function of, say, the novelist. But if once the liaison I foresee is established between criticism and psychology, then the individualist in dramatic art will find how probing the instruments of criticism can be.

§ 4

Lessing's cautious response to the naturalism of Diderot is shown in other ways. But in some measure he can accept the new ideas readily, because though for Diderot they may express an immediate revolt against the absurdities of Voltaire, for Lessing they are more than this: they are a return to the "infallible principles". Thus "Diderot is not wrong in pronouncing his thoughts on the superfluity and poverty of all uncertain expectations and sudden surprises to be as new as they are valid. They are new in regard to their abstraction, but very old in regard to the patterns from which they are abstracted. . . ." But it is sad to observe that where Lessing and Diderot agree, the modern naturalists elect to differ. There is an almost total unawareness of this consideration in modern plays and in modern dramatic criticism. Suspense, sustained excitement, surprise, and innocent deception are the foundations of the modern playwright's craft. And this craft is, of course, but one more reflection of the extensive vulgarity of the modern mind. Lessing refers us to Euripides. Euripides was so certain of himself that he almost always showed his spectators the goal whither he would lead them. The gratification of a childish curiosity was the least of the pretensions of his art. His aim was to awaken emotions in the spectator "not so much by that which should occur, as by the mode in which it should occur". Can the modern dramatists appreciate that distinction? Can they understand that art does not begin until interest is at an end? But why make this rhetorical pretence? There is no question. The dramatist is no longer a poet: the *mode* of art is not even a consideration for him. His aim is to satisfy an interest, to "pander" to a curiosity; above all to supply a commercial article to be played in a commercial theatre before a commercial audience. The circle is complete. Every interest is satisfied and the dissentient voice is half-ashamed of its lonely reverberations.

§ 5

A minor agreement between Lessing and Diderot is found in the question of natural diction. Lessing could not deny that "every passion has its own eloquence". Aristotle would not deny it. And Lessing nowhere shows his sensible qualities so openly as in this simple acceptance of Diderot's attitude. The least inclination to pedantry or conservativism would have caused him to halt here; but the criterion, in this and equally in his acceptance of Aristotle, was logic and common-sense. "There can never be feeling with a stilted, chosen, pompous language. It is not born of feeling, it cannot evoke it. But feeling agrees with the simplest, commonest, plainest words and expressions. . . ." And here for once Lessing and Diderot have little to teach the modern dramatist, who has not added pomposity or affectation of language to his other faults. But it is a negative virtue: he is not pompous nor is he ever sublime.

§ 6

The main energy of Lessing, however, was reserved for a restatement of Aristotle's theory of *catharsis*. Here again one may feel an absence of relevance in this "Serbonian bog" of criticism. Does Aristotle's theory mean anything to-day, in modern terms? Has it any bearing at all on the function of modern drama?

Lessing realized that the only justification for drama as a distinct form of art lay in its direct appeal to social emotions. The poem and the prose fiction, on the other hand, operate individually. Aristotle's theory—that the function of drama is the correction and refinement of the emotions of pity and fear—is based on the psychological fact that these emotions are most thoroughly excited—are, in fact, only complete—when aroused in a social unit: the unanimous group, the representative herd. That at any rate must be the modern justification for Aristotle's empirical selection of these two particular emotions. What Aristotle meant by the process of catharsis is precisely the point upon which so much wasted intellect has been expended. The view adopted by Lessing, and the only reasonable view at the time, was that by vicarious experience our pity and our fear, and all connected with them, become "purified". In Lessing's day there was no science of human behaviour adequate to account for either the process or the result. But modern psychology could, I think, give a fairly acceptable explanation—one that would not only restore the theory of Aristotle to its former standing, but would add fresh significance to this extraordinarily prescient hypothesis and reinstate it as a final criterion. It would reason that the instincts of pity and fear are primal instincts of man in his social aggregation; that these instincts in a healthy community must have expression; that direct expression is denied by the elaborate manners of civilization; and that vicarious expression can and must be given imaginary play. The drama thus becomes a sublimation of social instincts: a safety-valve against undue pressures on the fabric of civilization.

§ 7

We see how tolerantly, in these various gages, Lessing holds the balance between the extreme naturalism of Diderot (with its wider reverberations in the theories of Rousseau) and the fine logic of Aristotle's system. Lessing's great achievement, in fact, was to direct the growing turbulence of romanticism towards the static truths of classical dogma. "In nature", he wrote in one of his most significant passages, "everything is connected, everything is interwoven, everything changes with everything, everything merges from one into another. But such endless variety (*unendlicher Mannichfaltigkeit*) is only a play for an infinite spirit. In order that finite spirits may have their share of this enjoyment, they must have the power to set up arbitrary limits; they must have the power to eliminate and to guide their attention at will. This power we exercise at all moments of our life; without this power there would be no life for us; from too many various feelings we should feel nothing, we should be the constant prey of present impressions, we should dream without knowing what we dream. The purpose of art is to save us this abstraction in the realms of the beautiful and to render the fixing of our attention easy to us. All in nature that we might wish to abstract in our thoughts from an object or a combination of various objects, be it in time or in place, art really abstracts for us, and accords us this object or this combination of various objects as purely and tersely as the sensations they are to provoke allow."

Diderot had a mere glimmering of these truths. but it was a real light. " Nature may indeed have her sublime moments; but I think if anyone can be sure of seizing their sublimity and fixing it, it is he who has plumbed them with imagination or with genius, and has then expressed them with *sang-froid*" (*Paradoxe sur le Comédien*).

Lessing's attitude prepared the way for Goethe, Lessing in many ways made Goethe possible.

But the *sang-froid* of Diderot? It was engulfed not only in Diderot's own chaos, but in the unrestrained tide for which he, in his way, was the precursor. In the vortex that followed we see only one figure clutching at this frail straw of *sang-froid*: it is a frail straw, but it has carried Henri Beyle into modern consciousness and given his work a significance beyond the limits of his time.

§ 8

These rather random comments may perhaps now be drawn into relation with present issues. If I take William Archer as a representative disciple of Diderot, I do so quite alive to the dangers attending my choice. Archer's opinions, expressed so forcibly in the book which we may regard as the summary of his life's work,[1] are so sparkling with crotchets that there is a possibility of the critic's indignation spending itself on the unrelated opinions rather than on the essential errors that lie underneath. But I must select Archer not only because he was a most lively champion of modern drama (" modern " in a retrospective sense), but also because his work as a critic had a formative influence of considerable extent on that drama. He, more aptly than anyone else, denotes and personifies the period from 1890 to 1920—a period of genuine activity and

[1] *The Old Drama and the New: an Essay in Re-valuation.* London, 1923.

undoubtedly of healthy renewal, but a period also, surely, of dreadful limitations. But these limitations did not exist for Archer: he honestly thought the generation of Pinero, Barrie, Shaw, and Galsworthy probably superior to any other generation of playwrights in the history of English literature. And his prejudice did not spring from lack of knowledge—but did perhaps spring from too much knowledge of a specialized kind.

Shakespeare was a great inconvenience to Archer: Shakespeare had always to be made an exception to his bold generalizations—to all save one, for Shakespeare, despite his greatness as a poet, is not to be considered so intelligent or thought-provoking as Mr. Shaw or Mr. Galsworthy. He was a " stupendous genius " but *not* a " colossal intellect "—a distinction I fail to make, though Archer says they are " totally different things ". Shakespeare was " content to live in a stationary world "; he was not " alive to the great idea which differentiates the present age from all that have gone before—the idea of progress ". Here Archer betrays himself. This " great idea ", unknown to Shakespeare—was it not equally unknown to Aeschylus and Euripides, to Racine and Molière? Was it, in fact, known to anyone before Diderot and Rousseau invented it and an evolutionary philosophy perfected it? This is not the place to discuss the merits of the idea of progress: I would merely suggest that as an idea it has no more special precedence, apart from the cupidity of human desires, than any other idea—the idea of fatality, for example, or the idea of eternal recurrence. To think otherwise only betrays the humanistic prejudices on which this attitude of William Archer's is based, and from which his other more particular prejudices take their shape.

Our representative modernist lays down three tests of dramatic worth. One, that drama should say and mean something, does not need discussion: to anyone but a "pure aesthete" it is a test too obvious to be in question. The second test requires an affirmative answer to the following question:

"Is the story developed, and are the characters presented, in such a way as to make the best use of the mechanism of the theatre, and to beget in the audience, in high intensity, those emotions of growing interest, suspense, anticipation, sudden and vivid realization, which it is the peculiar privilege of drama to produce?"

I have already dealt with the notion of suspense. Aesthetically it seems to me to involve a vulgar intention and for that reason I believe it was obviated by the classical dramatists. The other matter involved in this test—the full use of the mechanism of the theatre—I also believe to be beset with error. I think it should be an incontrovertible principle that the drama dictates to the theatre and not the theatre to the drama. That a poet should ignore the *essentials* of the stage is, of course, folly; but these essentials are extremely simple and extremely obvious. The rest is technical obscurantism. The attitude is usually bolstered up by the classical instances of Shakespeare and Molière—both actors and stage-managers and *therefore* good playwrights. But an occasional coincidence does not prove a rule or sanction a generalization. A host of utterly banal playwright-actors and playwright-managers weigh down the scale against Shakespeare and Molière. The real danger underlying this demand is that the imagination should be intimidated by the technicalities of stage machinery and by the supposed necessity of any mechanical or conventional properties. But this question is closely related to that involved in Archer's first and most insistent test.

"The theatre of all ages", he writes, "is a machine devised, or rather developed, for the purpose of presenting to an assemblage of human beings imitations of human life, and thereby awakening a certain order of emotions which cannot be aroused in an equal degree by any other means". That this won't do as a definition of Greek tragedy is obvious even to Mr. Archer: he therefore makes the baffling distinction that "Greek tragedy was not a realistic, but a consistent, imitation". This is again a distinction without a difference—or rather, the words fail to express any distinction at all; they merely avoid the issue. In what possible sense can an imitation be realistic and not consistent? The point need not be pressed, for though he neglects the difficulty presented by Greek tragedy, Mr. Archer has no hesitation in applying his test to our own Elizabethan drama. The result is bloody in the extreme: not a reputation—" Shakespeare apart "—survives the ordeal.

That two centuries have been totally astray; that intelligences as acute as Lamb's, Coleridge's, and Swinburne's were utterly at sea; that the modern apologists for the Elizabethans are mere " aesthetic paradox-mongers "—all these things are possible. But they are not likely, and Archer had not the gift of persuading people either by imaginative expression or logical argument. His fallacy seems to begin with a strange historical misconception of the use of the word " imitation ": he gave it the sense (and the epithet) of *pure* imitation, and by this implied the exactest photographic and phonographic representationalism—no other words will suffice for his extraordinarily bourgeois conception. Only a radical misunderstanding of the very nature of art could have supported him in the long analysis he made on the basis of his blind theory. He did not understand that all truly imaginative art " functions " at a remove from reality. As in painting the artist selects from the disordered elements present in his direct vision, working his selected details into some pattern or abstraction, so in literature the poet creates his formal design, his stylized expression.

Because his instinct is to " create ", his materials must be " plastic "—his will is free. Archer, of course, saw that there was a difference, quality for quality, between the old drama and the new; this difference he ascribed to " passion " and " exaggeration " expressed in lyrical poetry; this poetry he thought he could dissociate entirely from the drama; and the dramatic essentials " left over " were—pure imitation, technical efficiency, intellectual content. But it is not merely a question of occasional lyric utterance: modern drama, though it may answer to Archer's three essentials, and though it may eschew lyric utterance, lacks something else. It lacks the power to transmute its materials; it burns at a low temperature and with little light. It does not lift us into that other world which is the world of imaginative logic. That world is only seen when habitual ways are stopped, when the unwitting receptivity of sights and sounds is replaced by a heightened awareness of the unreal reality of existence. Then the mind of the inspired dancer does indeed become identified with his god.[1]

[1] " It is very tempting ", writes Mr. Archer in a note, " to identify *imitation* with the Greek *mimesis* (applied in the main to the *ethos*, or character, of ordinary human beings). . . . But it appears on enquiry that the Greek words have no exact equivalent in English . . . *mimesis* meant originally 'the state of mind of the inspired dancer representing or becoming his god. . . .' " (*The Old Drama and the New*, p. 4).

VII

THE DEFINITION OF COMEDY

RATHER more than a hundred years ago Hazlitt, in his *Lectures on the English Comic Writers*, first used the word " artificial " in speaking of Congreve. Charles Lamb immediately afterwards gave the word, in the same connexion, a currency of charm and fashion. From that day to this—the day of Sir Edmund Gosse and the reviewers who slavishly follow where he misleads—the word " artificial " has sufficed to explain Congreve and the school of comedy which he brought to perfection. It should be noted straightaway that the word is used in a commendatory, or at least an apologetic sense. Hazlitt thought the character of Millamant " better adapted for the stage " (than that of Imogen or Rosalind) because " it is more artificial, more theatrical, more meretricious ". Lamb, developing this suggestion, excused what he really thought an indulgence " beyond the diocese of the strict conscience " by ascribing to the comedies of Wycherley and Congreve (in an essay by very name on the *Artificial* Comedy) an imaginary " land of cuckoldry—the Utopia of gallantry, where pleasure is duty, and the manners perfect freedom ". Comedy thus became for him an inverse sort of idealism, in which actions and sentiments had their being on a plane quite removed from actuality, and therefore quite remote in influence.

Hazlitt and Lamb were in a real dilemma. They had boundless admiration for the wit and artistry of these comedies, but they could not reconcile them with the moral consciousness of their own age. Or, if this seems to put too much stress on *moral* consciousness, very much the same difficulty was involved by the romantic consciousness then equally rife. The moral code would balk at the profligacy of Wycherley's and Congreve's characters: the romantic code, in mute conspiracy, would shy at the cynical realism with which these authors treated the passion of love, or the feminine mind. Therefore a process known to the psychologist as " rationalization " supervened, and the theory of artificial comedy was elaborated. It was a plausible idea, and the dilemma was effectively shelved in the subconscious mind.

By 1841 the moral consciousness had stiffened. The Victorian age was in full vigour, and Macaulay, writing in that year, was able to dismiss Lamb's theory of artificial comedy as " altogether sophistical "—not because he thought such a theory derogatory to the literary merits of the plays in question, but because he felt it to be a lame defence of a literature inherently perverse and corrupted.

" In the name of art, as well as in the name of virtue, we protest against the principle that the world of pure comedy is one into which no moral enters. If comedy be an imitation, under whatever conventions, of real life, how is it possible that it can have no reference to the great rule which directs life, and to feelings which are called forth by every incident of life? . . . But it is not the fact that the world of these dramatists is a world into which no moral enters. Morality constantly enters into that world, a sound morality, and an unsound morality; the sound morality to be insulted, derided, associated with everything mean and hateful; the unsound morality to be set off to every advantage, and inculcated by all methods, direct and indirect."

And so on. With Macaulay's main contention we agree. The world of our comic dramatists *is* real, and is meant to be real. Lamb's argument *is* altogether sophistical. But Macaulay's is something worse. It is heterodox criticism of the most subversive type. It is the utter confusion of morality and art. "The question", says Macaulay, "is simply this, whether a man of genius who constantly and systematically endeavours to make this sort of character attractive, by uniting it with beauty, grace, dignity, spirit, a high social position, popularity, literature, wit, taste, knowledge of the world, brilliant success in every undertaking, does or does not make an ill use of his powers. We own that we are unable to understand how this question can be answered in any way but one." But this, as applied to Congreve, and even to Wycherley, is a misstatement of the position and a misunderstanding of the men. But before we can answer Macaulay's question, in a way he would be unable to understand, we must be clear as to what we intend by the function of comedy.

The distinction between wit and humour, which is the first essential of the matter, has often been attempted, but, except in a few sharp phrases of Meredith's, with no very satisfactory results. Hazlitt's antitheses are merely descriptive, and in the manner of such criticism, end insignificantly. " Humour is the describing the ludicrous as it is in itself; wit is the exposing it, by comparing it or contrasting it with something else. Humour is, as it were, the growth of nature and accident; wit is the product of art and fancy. Humour, as it is shewn in books, is an imitation of the natural or acquired absurdities of mankind, or of the ludicrous in accident, situation and character; wit is the illustrating and heightening the sense of that absurdity by some sudden and unexpected likeness or opposition of one thing to another, which sets off the quality we laugh at or despise in a still more contemptible or striking point of view. . . . Wit hovers round the borders of the light and trifling, whether in matters of pleasure or pain. . . . Wit is, in fact, the eloquence of indifference. . . ."

Hazlitt also makes use of Congreve's own conception of humour as " a singular and unavoidable manner of doing or saying anything, Peculiar and Natural to one Man only; by which his Speech and Actions are distinguished from those of other Men " (Letter to Mr. Dennis concerning Humour in Comedy). But this is using " humour " in the rather special sense given to it by Ben Jonson, and does not really touch the distinction between humour and wit. Such a " humour " is rather the object on which humour in the general sense may be exercised. We must adopt some more precise distinction.

I would suggest one that may be readily used: humour differs from wit in the degree of action implied; or, to express the same idea psychologically, in the degree of introversion or extraversion expressed. The more the comic spirit resorts to activity or accident to gain its point, the more it tends to humour; and, in the contrary direction, the more the comic spirit seeks to achieve its effect in abstract or intellectual play, the better it merits the term wit. This distinction implies a no-man's-land where the categories overlap; and as a matter of fact it is in such a no-man's-land that some of the best English comedies, such as Wycherley's *Country Wife* and *Plain Dealer*, have their peculiar existence.

This pragmatical distinction conforms to the guiding idea of Meredith's *Essay on Comedy*—the idea of comedy as the humour of the mind.

" The comic poet is in the narrow field, or enclosed square of the society he depicts; and he addresses the still narrower enclosure of men's intellects, with reference to the operation of the social world upon their characters. [And again:] The Comic, which is the perceptive, is the governing spirit, awakening and giving aim to the powers of laughter, but it is not to be confounded with them: it enfolds a thinner form of them, differing from satire, in not sharply driving into the quivering sensibilities, and from humour, in not comforting them and tucking them up. . . ."

But it is time to return to Macaulay—and then to Congreve. Macaulay's moral outburst will now be seen to involve a misconception of comedy and indeed of all art. It is also based on a misstatement of fact: The "morality" of Congreve's plays is far from being that of "low town-rakes" and "dashing Cyprians". One could search in vain, even in the sort of literature approved by Macaulay, for characters more agreeable than Valentine and Angelica, or indeed, for a play more generally salutary in its theme than *Love for Love*. In *The Double Dealer* the true lovers, Mellefont and Cynthia, are perfect exemplars of virtue, vigorously contrasted against the villainy of Maskwell and Lady Touchwood. The conventional propriety of the Mourning Bride has never been questioned, except by Jeremy Collier, who descends to the lowest level of his crassness in the attempt. Voltaire's astonishment at the "cleanness" of Congreve is well known. But this kind of justification, though possible, is otiose. Art is a general activity, and any limitations to its scope are meaningless and arbitrary. It includes in its field of vision the immoral as well as the moral—and all other qualities of the human mind. The question of values is relative, and only concerns the artist in a formative sense; and such values are the general values of culture, among which the moral values have no special precedence. They are part of that perceptive sense which is the fund of character; and it is the quality of the artist's mind, as Henry James said,[1] that determines the deepest quality of his art. But to require, in the manner of Macaulay, that the artist's moral conscience should sit in judgement as his characters take shape in his imagination, is a stupidity of the most elementary kind, showing a complete misunderstanding of the function of art and of the psychology of the artist. It was the same stupidity that caused Macaulay to heap ridiculous praise on Collier's *Short View of the Immorality and Profaneness of the English Stage*, "... whose hysterical screaming and scoldings were to some degree perpetuated by being condensed in the vapid and lack-lustre philippics of one who was both pedant and prig, Thomas Babington Macaulay ".[2]

There is every evidence that Congreve was no mere genius of the instinctive order, but a critical writer fully conscious of the nature of his powers. I have already quoted from the Letter to Dennis; there are more passages of the same nature to be

[1] *Cf.* p. 219.

[2] Mr. Montague Summers, in his Introduction to *The Complete Works of William Congreve*. London, 1923, p. 30.

culled. In his reply to Collier's attack, Congreve fell back on the Aristotelian definition of comedy as " an Imitation of the worst sort of People . . . in respect to their Manners ". Again, in the Dedication of the *Double Dealer* he had replied to the accusation that he represented some Women as vicious and affected in these words:

" How can I help it? It is the business of a Comick poet to paint the Vices and Follies of Humane kind; and there are but two sexes that I know, viz. *Men* and *Women*, which have a Title to Humanity: And if I leave one half of them out, the work will be imperfect. I should be very glad of an opportunity to make my Complement to those Ladies who are offended; but they can no more expect it in a Comedy than to be Tickled by a Surgeon when he's letting 'em blood. They who are Virtuous or Discreet should not be offended, for such Characters as these distinguish them, and make their Beauties more shining and observ'd: And they who are of the other kind, may nevertheless pass for such, by seeming not to be displeased or touched with the Satyr of this *Comedy*."

This is very like Meredith's spirit of Comedy. The weakness, if weakness there is, lies in the word *satire*—not that it is used by Congreve with any special deliberation. But it marks a certain lack of perception, least noticeable in Congreve among all his contemporaries, but still present. " Our English school ", writes Meredith, " has not clearly imagined society; and of the mind hovering above congregated men and women, it has imagined nothing." Further on in the same Essay, Meredith quotes Landor: "'Genuine humour and true wit require a sound and capacious mind, which is always a grave one'," and he then remarks: "Congreve had a certain soundness of mind; of capacity, in the sense intended by Landor, he had little." This charge is well placed and skilfully supported by chapter and verse; and must for the present be recorded as the final word on Congreve. Of Congreve's character we derive from his letters and from contemporary accounts a fairly real conception; it lives best in Swift's epithet "unreproachful". But it adds nothing to the critical question. Of his mind we know less. From such writings as the *Amendments to Mr. Collier's False and Imperfect Citations* and the *Discourse on the Pindarique Ode* we can judge it to have been learned and even a little pedantic. His lack of capacity would seem to have been rather in the nature of a defect of vision. But vision is an idle word which we must try to make a little more precise.

The comic spirit, in Meredith's sense, is subject to three declensions or diminutions of effect. It can become, as Satire, angry and acidulated—an instrument of invective and not of persuasion. It can become, as Irony, indirect and uncertain. And as Humour it can identify itself with its object, revelling in the situation rather than offering any solution of it. Congreve is alert enough not to stray into any of these by-ways of the comic spirit; but it cannot be said that his conceptions are always " purely comic, addressed to the intellect ". The epithet that fits them best is *cynical* : it is not the calm curious eye of Meredith's spirit, but the calm *in*curious eye appropriate to another attitude.

Of cynicism one can say little but that it is the spirit of comedy without gravity, without profundity. When we pass from Congreve to Molière, or even to Meredith himself, we have left an arid for a rich amusement. Perhaps there are epochs in history, as certainly there are periods in life, when no attitude but cynicism is possible, because despair is too inevitable. And perhaps the end of the Seventeenth Century was such an epoch, as our own day seems to be another. In any case, such a supposition would go far to explain the only defect of Congreve's comedy, and whilst explaining it, make it forgiveable.

But in the process of explanation we must never forget the real achievement. Congreve's quality at its best, in *The Way of the World*, is of a texture, undeniably intellectual, that baffles the would-be analyst. To begin with, it is impossible to trace it down to a passage or a phrase. It lives in the characters, who are created by suggestion rather than by description. It becomes more a matter of localized fact in the extremely efficient and finely rhythmed style. This one might illustrate at random from any of the four comedies.

A soliloquy of Mirabell's from *The Way of the World* will serve (Millamant has just left him with a " when you have done thinking of that, think of me "):

" *Mira.* I have something more—Gone—Think of you! To think of a Whirlwind, tho' 'twere in a Whirlwind, were a Case of more steady Contemplation; a very tranquility of Mind and Mansion. A Fellow that lives in a Whirlwind, has not a more whimsical Dwelling than the Heart of a Man that is lodg'd in a Woman. There is no Point of the Compass to which they cannot turn, and by which they are not turn'd; and by one as well as by another; for Motion not Method is their Occupation. To know this, and yet continue to be in Love, is to be made wise from the Dictates of Reason, and yet persevere to play the Fool by the force of Instinct.—O here come my pair of Turtles—What, billing so sweetly! Is not Valentine's Day over with you yet? "

I have selected this passage for the perfect management of transitions, for the mastery of phrase, and for the apt use of rhythm and alliteration; but I doubt if I could find a better one to illustrate the real basis of thought, or, as we should perhaps say nowadays, of psychological observation, that after all sets Congreve's comedies apart from those of his contemporaries, not excepting even Wycherley. The oppositions of Motion and Method, of Reason and Instinct, though embodied in comic play, are not there by chance;

and for their date they strike a strangely modern note, a note that sounds again and again as we read through these plays, making Congreve significant to our own generation in a sense only shared by Donne among the English writers of the seventeenth century.

VIII

THE DIALOGUE

§ I

IT was Landor's opinion that " the best writers in every age have written in dialogue "; but it is curious how little, apart from the classifications of the Platonists, has been written *about* the dialogue. No attempt seems ever to have been made to define the principles of such a literary form; and while it is a method much used by a disciplined cast of mind, it has scarcely become one of classical precision. Perhaps if we were wise we should rejoice in one field left unmown by the blades of pedantry and logic; but categories are dear to the critic, and a short essay in eliminations may not be without interest to the general reader.

A cursory review of " the best writers " reveals a use of three distinct kinds of dialogue, agreeing only in the superficial appearance of the printed page. There is (i) the dialogue of ideas, in which the speakers are but embodiments of points of view; such a dialogue is exemplified in the characteristic work of Plato, Berkeley, Leopardi, Renan, and (to-day) M. Paul Valéry. To this category we might add, in so far as it ever becomes an artistic form, the dialogue of instruction, such as Fénelon's *Dialogues on Eloquence*. Next there is (ii) the dialogue of wit, which, though it has some idea in the background, tends not to expose this idea in the direct manner of Plato, but rather to get its effect indirectly by ironic ridicule or happy expression. This is the method of Lucian and of Fontenelle. Lastly there is (iii) the dialogue whose purpose is to exhibit character and personality; and this, of course, is the method largely practised by Landor.

It seems hopeless to reduce all this diversity to any common rationale or " dialogic ". But one principle at least is essential to all the methods, and is present from the very beginning of the form. Plato is said to have been inspired by the lost Sicilian mimes of Sophron and Epicharmus, but it is likely that he merely found there the suggestion and not the substance of the form. For we must at once recognize that in Plato the dialogue has been purged of its dramatic nature. The *Phaedo*, as a narrative, is intensely dramatic; as a dialogue it is a supreme example of de-dramatization. It is not merely that, as Jowett says, " no dialogue has a greater unity of subject and feeling "; but this effect is itself secured by the formal construction of the dialogue as such. It is, most notably, a dialogue within a dialogue: Phaedo, who was present at the death of Socrates, relates the events and discussions that accompanied it to Echecrates of Phlius. The " tragedy " is not merely given a distance in time and place, but is heard indirectly and through the channel of one unifying mind. We have, indeed, a sense of intense pathos, but it is abiding: it begins with the first words of Echecrates and ends only with that calm death and Phaedo's simple epitaph. The philosophical resignation of Socrates is like a key-note penetrating to the very essence of the aesthetic form in which it is embodied; till the dialogue itself is abstracted to a region of passionless integrity. Could any other form achieve this effect: give the same variety without expense of unity, and the same intensity with such evenness, such grace, such absence of melodramatic violence? But the *Phaedo* is too exceptional to be a pattern: it seems, in its plenitude and exactitude, to live on the very limits or boundaries of its form. The norm has a more definite nucleus: an extreme of formal necessities separated by a wide enough gap from neighbouring categories. And at the nucleus is the idea. The *Phaedo*, too, has its idea: there is not merely the motive or theme, which is the immortality of the soul, but there is the underlying assumption, common to all profound philosophies, but never so perfectly exemplified as here, that the service of abstractions must dominate the practice of life. But in the *Phaedo* there is, as we have seen, something more than the idea—there is a narrative. Yet for perfection the dialogue need not have more than ideas. If the essential of drama is the portrayal of action, then the essential of dialogue is the creative activity of ideas—ideas in action, one might say. But not embodied action itself. In this fact is the first and most distinct principle of the art.

But merely to contrast action and ideas is perhaps not enough in the way of distinction. When we descend to the actual construction of a form of literary composition, such as drama, we find that its essence is not so much in its subject-matter as in the manner of the treatment of that subject-matter. We come precisely to those questions of diction, stress, and rhythm so repugnant to the mere appreciator of literature, and so necessary to the real critic. It has recently been suggested in an ingenious dialogue,[1] which is in itself an illustration of our theme, that " what makes a work dramatic is not so much its obvious shape, as the structure of its changes of motion. . . . The dramatic moment is that at which a change of speed intrudes." This dynamic definition will suit our purpose very well. We shall lay it down as an axiom that the perfect dialogue has an evenness of motion within which the *dénouement* of ideas makes its maximum effect; its outer " speed " does not change, or only slightly, like the fountain that holds a ball in merry suspense.

Some happy chance or intuition has saved most of our authors from the dramatic fallacy. Diderot naturally, in his experimental fashion, comes nearest to disproving the principle. *Le Neveu de Rameau* illustrates as well as any other dialogue

[1] *Histriophone*, by Bonamy Dobrée. London, 1925.

the play and counterplay of ideas, but it is interspersed with elaborate " stage directions "—to a degree, in fact, quite foreign to drama. It rather approaches to narrative form, and has been credited with effect on the history of fiction. It is picturesque and human, and in some ways the most interesting of all Diderot's writings; but considered as a dialogue (it is rather a monologue) the form, aiming at the development of ideas or the revelation of character, is in no way heightened or quickened, but quite overladen, by its explanatory devices. But it is in some sort an anticipation of Landor, and for this reason is perhaps more interesting than the less original dialogues which Diderot wrote in the elenctic manner of Plato. These, however, we must not despise, for Diderot had wit as well as logic, and everywhere, but especially in *Le Rêve de D'Alembert* (and its audacious *Suite*), we have evidence of Fontenelle's happy influence.

In the dramatic category we should also reckon Swift's *Polite Conversation*, a dialogue ridiculing the cant phrases of the time; but it is not strictly speaking a dialogue of ideas, and the fact that though published simply as a literary dialogue, it was nevertheless actually staged, is sufficient evidence of its dramatic nature. In the dialogue to which we have already referred, Mr. Dobrée has much to say about the texture of dramatic dialogue, and pleads for a stage speech in which the changing speeds of the drama will be sensitively reflected—" a medium that can be at will swift, rhetorical or quiet . . . above all, a medium that shall be actor-proof, actor-easy, and clear, and which, though artificially made, shall sound on the stage as naturally rapid as the flowing of a stream". The medium for dialogue would agree with this in many respects: it would, of course, be artificial, for all speech that is lifted out of the casualness of natural conversation into the formal arrangement of art is in that degree artificial; actors it will ignore; but it will be clear to express ideas, apt for repartee, and not so much swift as rhetorical, and not so much rhetorical as quiet. It is perhaps impossible to illustrate these qualities except in a complete dialogue, but the following passage from the opening of *Hylas and Philonous* is not wanting in the obvious texture of this kind of writing:

" *Phil.* Good morning, Hylas: I did not expect to find you abroad so early.

" *Hyl.* It is indeed something unusual; but my thoughts were so taken up with a subject I was discoursing of last night, that, finding I could not sleep, I resolved to rise and take a turn in the garden.

" *Phil.* It happened well, to let you see what innocent and agreeable pleasures you lose every morning. Can there be a pleasanter time of the day, or a more delightful season of the year? That purple sky, those wild but sweet notes of birds, the fragrant bloom upon the trees and flowers, the gentle influence of the rising sun, these and a thousand nameless beauties of nature inspire the soul with secret transports; its faculties too, being at this time fresh and lively, are fit for these meditations, which the solitude of a garden and tranquillity of the morning naturally dispose us to. But I am afraid I interrupt your thoughts: for you seemed very intent on something.

"*Hyl.* It is true, I was, and shall be obliged to you if you will permit me to go on in the same vein; not that I would by any means deprive myself of your company, for my thoughts always flow more easily in conversation with a friend than when I am alone: but my request is, that you would suffer me to impart my reflections to you.

"*Phil.* With all my heart, it is what I should have requested myself if you had not prevented me.

"*Hyl.* I was considering the odd fate of those men who have in all ages, through an affectation of being distinguished from the vulgar, or some unaccountable turn of thought, pretended either to believe nothing at all, or to believe the most extravagant things in the world. This however might be borne, if their paradoxes and scepticism did not draw after them some consequences of general disadvantage to mankind. But the mischief lieth here; that when men of less leisure see them who are supposed to have spent their whole time in the pursuits of knowledge professing an entire ignorance of all things, or advancing such notions as are repugnant to plain and commonly received principles, they will be tempted to entertain suspicions concerning the most important truths, which they had hitherto held sacred and unquestionable.

"*Phil.* I entirely agree with you, as to the ill tendency of the affected doubts of some philosophers, and fantastical conceits of others. I am even so far gone of late in this way of thinking, that I have quitted several of the sublime notions I had got in their schools for vulgar opinions. And I give it you on my word, since this revolt from metaphysical notions to the plain dictates of nature and common sense, I find my understanding strangely enlightened, so that I can now easily comprehend a great many things which before were all mystery and riddle."

§ 2

Apart from the non-dramatic necessity, it is doubtful if any principle common to the three kinds of dialogue can be formulated. But it does remain to consider in what manner the three kinds fulfil their intentions. A platonic dialogue, such as the *Republic*, or such as Berkeley's *Alciphron*, proposes the logical establishment of a definite set of ideas; characters, imaginary, historical, or contemporary, are selected to personify points of view in relation to this body of ideas. Then the characters are " set ", and this " setting " of the dialogue is not unimportant: it creates an attitude of sympathy towards the subject of discourse or even serves as a base of reference for the illustration of ideas. In the *Phaedo* we saw it used to effect distance: but its general use is to effect atmosphere, as in Dryden's masterly way, in *An Essay of Dramatic Poesy.* The scene of this dialogue is composed to perfection, giving stillness after tumult, a rhythm of oars, and a gradual passage into the sphere of abstractions:

"It was that memorable day, in the first summer of the late war, when our navy engaged the Dutch; a day wherein the two most mighty and best appointed fleets which any age had ever seen, disputed the command of the greater part of the globe, the commerce of nations, and the riches of the universe. Whilst these vast floating bodies, on either side, moved against each other in parallel lines, and our countrymen under the happy conduct of his Royal Highness, went breaking, by little and little, into the line of the enemies; the noise of the cannon from both navies reached our ears about the City, so that all men being alarmed with it, and in a dreadful suspense of the event which we knew was then deciding, every one went following the sound as his fancy led him; and leaving the town almost empty, some took towards the park, some cross the river, others down it; all seeking the noise in the depth of silence.

"Among the rest it was the fortune of Eugenius, Crites, Lisideius, and Neander, to be in company together; three of them persons whom their wit and quality have made known to all the town; and whom I have chose to hide under these borrowed names, that they may not suffer by so ill a relation as I am going to make of their discourse.

" Taking then a barge which a servant of Lisideius had provided for them, they made haste to shoot the bridge, and left behind them that great fall of waters which hindered them from hearing what they desired; after which, having disengaged themselves from many vessels which rode at anchor in the Thames, and almost blocked up the passage towards Greenwich, they ordered the watermen to let fall their oars more gently; and then, every one favouring his own curiosity with a strict silence, it was not long ere they perceived the air break about them like the noise of distant thunder, or of swallows in a chimney: those little undulations of sound, though almost vanishing before they reached them, yet still seeming to retain somewhat of their first horror, which they had betwixt the fleets."

A dialogue that begins so naturally proceeds evenly; perhaps the convention of a scene may be kept up, as when Philonous stops to pluck a cherry and demonstrate that it is " nothing but a congeries of sensible impressions "; and usually a dialogue will end with some reversion to its setting, perhaps closing on a note of realism, as Dryden's does, with the party landing at the foot of Somerset Stairs and making their way " through a crowd of French people, who were merrily dancing in the open air, and nothing concerned for the noise of guns which had alarmed the town that afternoon."

The purpose of the dialogue is, we have contended, the expression of ideas; and a certain type of writer will resort to this form because it offers, as no other form can, the vivid presentation of opposing tenets. It must be confessed that some writers, without a mind on a subject, have thus used the form to expatiate on ideas which have no outcome. To be fair to both sides of a question is a laudable ambition, but it does not result in good literature. The vivid writer is the passionate one, even the prejudiced one; and the best dialogues of the expository kind lead to a decision. The logical proof is illustrated by the defeat in argument of the opponents of the thesis; and the resulting effect on the reader is ever so much more exhilarating than if he had merely read through a direct exposition. For one thing, rhetoric comes naturally at the crisis of an argument, and rhetoric in a due place will yield a heightened beauty of expression and a fine force of effect. For this reason the *Essay of Dramatic Poesy* is justly held to be the finest example of Dryden's prose; and it is impossible to insist too strongly on the pure literary quality of *Hylas and Philonous* and of *Alciphron*. Under the influence of the form of the dialogue, Berkeley's style, almost the purest and serenest in English literature, takes on an unrivalled precision and beauty.

§ 3

The quality of the second (which is Lucian's) kind of dialogue is rather indefinable, and is best approached by a quotation from Diderot's *Rêve de D'Alembert*:

" *Mademoiselle de l'Espinasse*. . . . Docteur, qu'est-ce que c'est que le sophisme de l'éphémère?

" *Bordeu*. C'est celui d'un être passager qui croît à l'immortalité des choses.

" *Mademoiselle de l'Espinasse*. La rose de Fontenelle qui disait que de mémoire de rose on n'avait vu mourir un jardinier?

" *Bordeu*. Précisément; cela est léger et profond."

Léger et profond! It is the secret of all art. We are reminded of Nietzsche's emphatic phrase: What is good is easy; everything divine runs with light feet. It is this secret that perpetuates the charm of Lucian and of his later reincarnation, Bernard de Fontenelle. Not that Lucian and Fontenelle have much in common, apart from their secret. Lucian's method is gay ridicule, with nothing beyond but sanity and sensible worldliness. This " last great master of Attic eloquence and Attic wit " gave to the dialogue variety, but not a little at the expense of its dignity. Lucian was one of those destructive spirits whose only weapon is irony; he was, in addition, a rhetorician, practised in the elaboration of fictitious " cases ", and when he came to use the dialogue, he found his qualities conjoining happily in this literary form. The dialogue enabled him to express that detachment of observation essential to irony, and it enabled him to present, almost dramatically, it must be confessed, the opposition of equal absurdities. Irony is the weapon of a second-rate writer, but it is not without its uses. It can demolish absurdities, pomposities, and vanities; and it can amuse an audience. Lucian is still very good reading, and he exists in an English translation which is itself a work of bounteous wit.[1] These translators have observed, in their introduction, that Lucian did not leave the dialogue as he found it; he profoundly modified its form. Beginning with an almost Platonic use, he only gradually came to a satiric use.

"That was an idea that we may suppose to have occurred to him after the composition of the 'Hermotimus'. This is in form the most philosophic of his dialogues. . . . The dialogue that, perhaps, comes next, 'The Parasite', is still Platonic in form, but only as a parody; its main interest . . . is in the combination for the first time of satire with dialogue. One more step remained to be taken. . . . It was the fusing of Comedy and Dialogue—the latter being the prose conversation that had hitherto been confined to philosophical discussion. The new literary form, then, was con-

[1] *The Works of Lucian of Samosata*, translated by H. W. Fowler and F. G. Fowler. In Four Volumes. Oxford (Clarendon Press), 1905.

versation, frankly for purposes of entertainment, as in Comedy, but to be read and not acted."

This brings us back to technical distinctions. It is an exact description of Lucian's method and reveals what, on any strict regard for the purity of the form, we must consider as his weakness. For in adopting his conversational tone Lucian deliberately abandoned the artifice of art. Conversation to be read (not acted) is really a contradiction in terms; at any rate, it is a confusion of terms. Conversation has its place in naturalistic narrative, but as a *literary* means it does not rightly exist. From the same confusion all "conversational" criteria of prose style break down: art, it can never be too often repeated, is discipline, definiteness, abstraction from chaos. Conversation is liberal, easy, redundant, organically natural; and the art that apes conversation partakes of its formless qualities.

It is the distinction of Fontenelle that, while following Lucian in the variety and subtlety of his particular method, he yet contrived to give his dialogues a texture of stylistic dignity and to endow them with intellectual complexity. Lucian, for all his gifts, tends to be a little banal. Not so Fontenelle. He is an obscure and enticing author, attracting the sympathetic mind to strong affections and irrational loyalty. His calm intelligence, equally devoid of enthusiasms and prejudices, perhaps came naturally and of necessity to this only perfectly detached form of writing. The form was made for a man of his temperament—not poet, not scientist, but *homme de lettres*, a subtle spirit standing between the worlds of knowledge and sensibility. His intellectual graces give him a certain solidity which is lacking in Lucian, and this he has without any loss of wit. In this solidity is his main distinction; but instead of the anomalous word " solidity " we might venture on " purpose ". " Tous vos Dialogues ", he writes in his dedication of the *Nouveaux Dialogues des Morts* to Lucian (" aux Champs Elisiens "), " renferment leur moral, et j'ay fait moraliser tous mes Morts; autrement ce n'eût pas esté la peine de les faire parler; des Vivans auroient suffi pour dire des choses inutiles." In the same place Fontenelle, writing of Lucian's style, distinguishes " cette simplicité fine, et cet enjouement naïf, qui sont si propres pour le Dialogue "—thus showing his deliberate conception of the form. Lucian had purpose too, as Fontenelle says, but it is merely the moral purpose of the leveller and satirist. Fontenelle himself had more, for he had a positive intellectual aim. He is the exponent of Descartes and Leibniz, and by giving a literary flavour to the new " experimental philosophy " (a term which he invented), he became, in Faguet's neat phrase, " le père discret et prudent " of the whole eighteenth century.

§ 4

It was left to Landor to elaborate the third kind of dialogue. *Imaginary Conversations* is not an idle synonym for "Dialogues", but describes more precisely the nature of the adopted *genre*. Landor was a classical writer in a romantic age, but he could not quite escape the influence of his environment. You can get a very exact contrast between his and Fontenelle's method by comparing *The Maid of Orleans and Agnes Sorel* with *Agnès Sorel et Roxelane*. Both writers proposed to illustrate the same theme—the influence of women on the affairs of men—and both selected Agnes Sorel as an embodiment of the idea. In Fontenelle's dialogue Agnes and Roxelane discuss the subject, illustrating it from their own experiences, and the moral of the dialogue is driven home in the climax of the argument:

"*A. Sorel.* J'avoue qu'il est beau d'assujettir ceux qui se précautionnent tant contre notre pouvoir.

"*Roxelane.* Les hommes ont beau faire; quand on les prend par les passions, on les mène où l'on veut. Qu'on me fasse revivre, et qu'on me donne l'Homme du monde le plus impérieux; je feray de luy tout ce qu'il me plaira, pourveu que j'aye beaucoup d'esprit, assez de beauté, & peu d'amour."

Landor's procedure is very different. He seizes on the romantic legend of Jeanne d'Arc's pleading with Agnes to use her love to awaken the King's latent patriotism; and he puts this scene, in all but rubrics, into dramatic form:

" *Jeanne*. I am so ignorant, I know only a part of my duties; yet those which my Maker has taught me I am earnest to perform. He teaches me that divine love has less influence over the heart than human; he teaches me that it ought to have more: finally, he commands me to announce to thee, not his anger, but his will.

" *Agnes*. Declare it; O declare it. I do believe his holy word is deposited in thy bosom.

" *Jeanne*. Encourage the king to lead his vassals to the field.

" *Agnes*. When the season is milder.

" *Jeanne*. And bid him leave you for ever.

" *Agnes*. Leave me! one whole campaign! one entire summer! Oh anguish! It sounded in my ears as if you had said ' for ever '.

" *Jeanne*. I say it again.

" *Agnes*. Thy power is superhuman, mine is not.

" *Jeanne*. It ought to be, in setting God at defiance. The mightiest of the angels rued it.

" *Agnes*. We did not make our hearts.

" *Jeanne*. But we can mend them.

" *Agnes*. Oh! mine (God knows it) bleeds.

" *Jeanne*. Say rather it expels from it the last stagnant drop of its rebellious sin. Salutary pangs may be painfuller than mortal ones.

" *Agnes*. Bid him leave me! wish it! permit it! think it near! believe it ever can be! Go, go . . . I am lost eternally."

Apart from the Landorian phrasing, which is fashioned and beautiful, the method is naturalistic, evocative of the sentimental associations of the scene. In Landor's case the theme is staged, in Fontenelle's it is stated, with precision and an effect of finality. Landor's method is the freshest, the least exploited, the most lavish in its possibilities. And for these reasons it is likely to find the more practicians in the future. But it has its limitations, the greatest of which is confusion with dramatic form. The fear is that the "imaginary conversation" will merely dissipate on miniature drama energy that might be guided into more effective channels. For surrounding this later form, merging with its circumference, is the waste, the wilderness of anecdote.

Lucian's method is personal and must wait for a wit born to the manner; but the Platonic form is there for anyone with taste, intelligence, and ideas. Not long ago it showed all its suppleness, its beauty, and its philosophic grace in the *Eupalinos* of Monsieur Paul Valéry.[1] In this exquisite dialogue—curiously comparable in its subject-matter with the third dialogue of *Alciphron* —we get the use of that technical device already discovered by Plato and subsequently developed by Lucian and Diderot,[2] in which the unity of a

[1] *Eupalinos, ou L'Architecte*, précédé de *L'Ame et la Danse*, par Paul Valéry. Paris, 1923.

[2] And by Juvenal, in a solitary example (Satire IX). But this dialogue is in verse, a complication I have deliberately avoided in this essay.

dialogue is preserved but the number of points of view conveniently increased by the introduction of dialogue within dialogue—that is, a dialogue reported by one of the speakers. It is a detail, but another device used by Monsieur Valéry in *L'Ame et la Danse* (the companion dialogue to *Eupalinos*) is of great beauty and of unmatched subtlety. The speakers are represented witnessing a Greek dancer, and as they watch, discussing the nature of the soul, the dance, in its movement and its music, becomes a symbol of the soul, and as the dance " works out " so does the argument. It is a perfect union of thought and action, so intimately interlinked that there is no question of the dramatic fallacy—the drama is an enduring metaphor; the action is in the ideas.

IX

CHARLOTTE AND EMILY BRONTË

HEREDITY is a factor underlying and determining all other causes and effects within the term of a human life, but in ascribing any importance to it, we should be careful to distinguish rather sharply between intelligence or mental development, which is the product of natural selection in the race and of education in the individual, and what for want of another word we must call genius, which, when it is of any value, is intelligence directed into personal and wayward channels.[1] It is merely the instrument of genius—the brain considered as a muscle—that is susceptible to hereditary influences. The rest is the product of environment and chance—particularly of the psychological events introduced into life by human relationships.

[1] "Talents do not appear to depend upon the improvement of any special mental quality by continued practice, but they are the expression, and to a certain extent the by-product, of the human mind, which is so highly developed in all directions" (A. Weismann, *On Heredity*, 1883). See also the same scientist's *Thoughts upon the Musical Sense in Animals and Man* (1889), where the general conclusions would support the position taken up in the present essay. Weismann is, of course, out of fashion—perhaps out of date—but he may still be read for the acuteness of many of his observations.

Because of its historical remoteness, heredity remains the least tangible of influences, and the observed facts, in a case like that of the Brontë family, are far too unreliable and unsystematic to be of much use. We see two human strains, themselves the products of incalculable forces, that unite and give issue to genius. The process, one can persist in believing, is as natural as a chemical combination, but it is impossible to reduce it to an equation. We can at the best but point to tendencies and characteristics in the parent stock and hazard that these are some of the elements responsible—though even these are but vague, obvious elements with their more definite collaterals in physiological and psychological recesses.

In the case of the Brontës we have, on the one side, a stock of somewhat barbarous origin, culminating in a man of determination and capability, a man who " early gave tokens of extraordinary quickness and intelligence ". Patrick Brontë had opened a public school at the age of sixteen, and at the age of twenty-five was still ambitious enough to proceed to Cambridge, where he took his degree after four years' study. Mrs. Gaskell's rather picturesque description of his passionate nature has been discredited in some of its details, but enough remains of authentic evidence to evoke for us a grim puritanical mask, expressing, even while it repressed, the fires beneath. Mrs. Brontë brought characteristics which were of a more ordinary nature, though perhaps no less essential to the result. She was intelligent, placid, and ailing. Her delicate constitution passed to her children, and perhaps this factor, more than any one other, determined their neurotic tendency. A neurosis, however, is never of a direct physical origin: the psychical complement, too, must be sought, and perhaps the mother provided this also by her early death in 1821, when Charlotte was but five and Emily three years old. The strong instinctive link between mother and child is never thus abruptly broken without unseen compensations and reverberations. I tread on delicate ground here—ground I would willingly leave to the expert psychologist. The enormous body of childish writings still existing in Charlotte's case, but until recently withheld for its lack of literary qualities, may conceivably be of great significance from this point of view. I will merely suggest that we have in Charlotte's seemingly endless fictive evocations of the Duke of Wellington[1] a phantasy of a kind clearly delineated by the researches of psycho-analysts. "Charlotte's little stories", writes Mr. Shorter, "commence in her thirteenth year, and go on until she is twenty-three.

[1] "Charlotte's little stories commence in her thirteenth year, and go on until she is twenty-three. From thirteen to eighteen she would seem to have had one absorbing hero—the Duke of Wellington. Whether the stories be fairy tales or dramas of modern life, they all alike introduce the Marquis of Douro. . . . The length of some of these fragments is indeed incredible" (Clement Shorter, *The Brontës, Life and Letters*, 1908, p. 72).

From thirteen to eighteen she would seem to have had one absorbing hero—the Duke of Wellington. Whether the stories be fairy tales or dramas of modern life, they all alike introduce the Marquis of Douro." Interpretations of such a phantasy as this might differ: Adler would see in it an unconscious attempt on the part of the neurotic weakling to free herself from a feeling of inferiority[1] by the creation of a compensating ideal of superiority; whereas Jung would find the unconscious origin of such a hero phantasy quite specifically in a longing for the lost mother. But whatever interpretation is adopted, a sense of inferiority, of incompleteness, is seen as the essential character of the neurosis underlying the phantasy.

In the case of Emily the same causes produced a "masculine protest" of a more complex kind, showing, indeed, the typical features of what I think we must, with the psycho-analyst, call psychical hermaphroditism. The outward expression of this state was evident enough. In her childhood the villagers thought her more like a boy than a girl. "She should have been a man:

[1] There are many direct betrayals in Charlotte's correspondence of this deeply-felt sense of inferiority. The following passage from the reminiscences of her school friend, Mary Taylor, is significant: "She always showed physical feebleness in everything. She ate no animal food at school. It was about this time I told her she was very ugly. Some years afterwards I told her I thought I had been very impertinent. She replied, 'You did me a great deal of good, Polly, so don't repent of it.'"

a great navigator!" cried M. Heger, despite his horror of her intractability. Charlotte refers to "a certain harshness in her powerful and peculiar character". "Stronger than a man, simpler than a child, her nature stood alone." Yet Emily was not given to expressing herself by outward speech or action; she was sombre and reserved—was, in fact, of a shy, introspective cast; from which clue the psychologist will realize how much deeper and more powerful must have been the masculine assumptions of her mind. These found their fit expression, in due course, in *Wuthering Heights*, whose very peculiar merits show that mingling of the strong and the sweet which some critics make the criterion of all great works of the imagination, and which, in her case, was but the direct expression of her nature.

We might pass further, in illustration of our point, to the cases of Anne and Branwell. The former as an example of religious melancholy, and the latter as an example of disintegrated personality, offer familiar characteristics: they are true to type. But consideration of them is much less important, because it does not bear on a creative artist of much significance. It is sufficient to observe that though all four cases present very diverse symptoms, they are all traceable to the one cause: the early rupture of the maternal bond of affection and protection, the counteraction of a stern, impassive father, the formation of inferiority complexes in the children, and the consequent compensations by phantasy.

What it is now necessary to emphasize strongly, in concluding this psychological excursus, is that art is a triumph over neurosis; that though it originates in a neurotic tendency, it is a coming-out-against this tendency; and that in the case of the three sisters the sublimation was achieved. Their art is not neurotic in kind; no art is. It is only when we search for causes and origins (as we have a perfect right to do) that we discover the neurosis; in the effect, according to the measure of its success, all is health and harmony.

In dealing with these psychological questions we have, I think, emphasized the kind of environment that leaves the deepest mark on the formation of character and genius. But we are left with the environment of place, of locality. This influence is most in question in the case of Emily, that "nursling of the moors", and indeed her poems show, I think, the most intense rendering of the embodied presence of nature that anywhere exists in English literature.

> The earth that wakes *one* human heart to feeling
> Can centre both the worlds of Heaven and Hell.

In these two lines she reaches a climax in her philosophy of nature, and shows a depth of emotional perception that not even Wordsworth could command.

But the question of the immediate influence of natural scenes differs from this general evocation of the spirit of nature. There is about the moors of Yorkshire, where they yet remain, a quality that works on the mobile senses. Their sparseness and loneliness drive you to an intimacy with whatever life does exist there; a small thing like the scent of bog-myrtle can kindle a strong emotion. There is a severity in the unrelieved reach of gradual hill country; the eye drifts into distant prospects, seeks the sky-line that is not a line, but a subtle merging of tones; the human mind *is* perhaps heard more distinctly in this inorganic stillness—only when, however, it has learned to think, and to express its thoughts. The moors, like any other local endowment, are merely material for observation and perception, and if into their confines there happens to enter a mind of exceptional dimensions, this mind will use its environment to some purpose. Such was the case with Emily Brontë. Charlotte, writing that eloquent and penetrating Preface to the second edition of *Wuthering Heights*, expresses this fact with all her rhetorical force:

"*Wuthering Heights* was hewn in a wild workshop, with simple tools, out of homely materials. The statuary found a granite block on a solitary moor; gazing thereon, he saw how from the crag might be elicited a head, savage, swart, sinister; a form moulded with at least one element of grandeur—power. He wrought with a rude chisel, and from no model but the vision of his meditations."

You see how objective the attitude of the artist

is made. A more facile conception would have imbued the statuary with the moor's savage elements, and made the image but the reflection of an entranced imagination. But the vision of her meditations was the product of an applied mind; and that this fixed itself mainly on a rustic scene was but the result of chance limitations—limitations, however, which we do not regret, since they drove that vision so deeply into the heart of the subject.

A far more effective factor, both in the case of Emily and of Charlotte, was what we might call quite simply education, but which resolves, upon deeper analysis, into the personal influence of Constantin Heger. In Charlotte's case it seems that this aggressive intellect—masculine, fiery, compact—came opportunely to occupy the stronghold of the unconscious evacuated by the Duke of Wellington, whose lustre had no doubt waned with the growth of experience and intelligence. From the psychological point of view, that is all that need be said of a personal relationship which has been the subject of much speculation; though the intense nature that the hero worship was to assume, before the end of Charlotte's stay in Brussels, was, as I shall make out later, a determining experience in her life.

The immediate importance of this contact was its purely literary consequences. Charlotte and Emily learned the meaning of style—and style not in the English sense of picturesqueness, but in the

French sense of clarity and brevity. Spirits that were romantic, or at any rate Celtic, submitted to the discipline of a strictly Latin mind—Latin in its scepticism, its dryness, and its dignity. Mrs. Gaskell printed a *devoir* of Charlotte's, corrected by M. Heger, where the process may be seen in action. In the simple and halting French then at Charlotte's command we already experience the peculiar force and vividness of her evocations; but the corrections and marginal comments of M. Heger are the precepts, not of a schoolmaster, but of a master of the art of writing. " He told me ", relates Mrs. Gaskell, " that one day this summer [when the Brontës had been for about four months receiving instruction from him] he read to them Victor Hugo's celebrated portrait of Mirabeau, ' mais, dans ma leçon je me bornais à ce qui concerne *Mirabeau Orateur*. C'est après l'analyse de ce morçeau, considéré surtout du point de vue du fond, de la disposition, de ce qu'on pourrait appeler *la charpente* qu'ont été faits les deux portraits que je vous donne.' He went on to say that he had pointed out to them the fault in Victor Hugo's style as being exaggeration in conception, and, at the same time, he had made them notice the extreme beauty of his ' nuances ' of expression. They were then dismissed to choose the subject of a similar kind of portrait. This selection M. Heger always left to them; for ' it is necessary ', he observed, ' before sitting down to write on a subject, to have thoughts and feelings about it.

I cannot tell on what subject your heart and mind have been excited. I must leave that to you.' "

When Charlotte finally left the Heger institute at Brussels, some eighteen months after the composition of the *devoir* referred to, the intense desire to write, which had been hers since childhood, assumed a more definite urgency. It was not merely that she had perfected, under the Professor's care, the methods of self-expression; she had also endured a nervous crisis of an indefinite nature but of a deep effect. She herself (in a letter to Miss Wooler in 1846) described her state as *hypochondria*: "I endured it but a year and assuredly I can never forget the concentrated anguish of certain insufferable moments, and the heavy gloom of many long hours, besides the preternatural horrors which seemed to clothe existence and nature, and which made life a continual walking nightmare. Under such circumstances the morbid nerves can know neither peace nor enjoyment; whatever touches pierces them: sensation for them is suffering." Mrs. Gaskell pictures some of the circumstances of this period. Charlotte had been left during the *grandes vacances* in the great deserted pensionnat, with only one teacher for a companion. "This teacher, a Frenchwoman, had always been uncongenial to her; but, left to each other's sole companionship, Charlotte soon discovered that her associate was more profligate, more steeped in a kind of cold, systematic sensuality, than she had before imagined it possible for a human being to be; and her whole nature revolted from this woman's society. A low nervous fever was gaining upon Miss Brontë. She had never been a good sleeper, but now she could not sleep at all. Whatever had been disagreeable, or obnoxious, to her during the day, was presented when it was over with exaggerated vividness to her disordered fancy. . . . In the day-time, driven abroad by loathing of her companion and by the weak restlessness of fever, she tried to walk herself into such a state of bodily fatigue as would induce sleep. . . . The shades of evening made her retrace her footsteps—sick for want of food, but not hungry; fatigued with long continued exercise—yet restless still, and doomed to another weary, haunted night of sleeplessness." During one such anguished progress, she found herself before a confessional in Ste. Gudule's, and, her strong Protestant prejudices succumbing to what she calls "an odd whim", she abandoned herself to that psychopathic consolation. "I was determined to confess," she writes to Emily. "I actually did confess—a real confession." The vivid use she made of the incident, in *Villette*, is only the most obvious record of this spiritual climax; the complete pathological phase (where sensation, as she says, was suffering) constituted, I think, the fundamental experience upon which she built her whole conception of imaginative reality.[1]

[1] In considering this period of her life, though I ignore, I do not deny what the four letters from Charlotte to Constantin Heger, published by *The Times* in 1913, are a sufficient proof of: the importance of her feelings for Professor Heger in the

I have here used an epithet, "imaginative", which it is necessary to use at all times with care and generally to avoid. It is one of those epithets that normally cloak a lack of thought or a failure of analysis. Nevertheless, I think it will be found, when reduced to its definite limits, to connote a certain process in the mind of the creative writer for which no other more suitable term can be used. The merely descriptive distinction between the fancy and the imagination, which has so long served in the sphere of literary criticism, is no longer adequate. It is not based on any correlated psychological events; and even when the elements of fancy are excluded, we are left with no clear boundaries to which we can confine the activities of the imagination. It is merely a distinction, as Pater pointed out, between degrees of intensity. It would not, however, serve any useful purpose to import into literary criticism the purely technical conception of the imagination current in the old psychology, however precise such a use might be. We merely want a more definite understand-

causation of this pathological state. There can be no question of the existence, in her mind, of an appalling conflict between the strength of her emotion and the considerations—social, moral, and religious—which caused her to hide, even from herself, the nature of this emotion. The result was a decided "complex", and I should be disposed to agree with a psychologist who identified her whole neurotic condition at this period with such a specific repression. I do not consider the *cause* of her state too closely because all I am concerned with is its effect upon her creative mind.

ing of the way in which ideas and images are associated in that abnormal manner we term imaginative. It was in the capture of such states of excitement that Wordsworth quite rightly saw the function of the poet. And although in the case of fiction the plane of conception is different, being more relative, less absolute; a detailed construction of dramatic events rather than a generalized expression of states of consciousness or thought; nevertheless, the psychological mechanism is the same. True imagination is a kind of logic; it is the capacity to deduce from the nature of an experienced reality, the nature of other unexperienced realities. And upon the depth and totality of the original experience will depend the reach and validity of the imaginative process. And if the process is kept to a quasi-logical rigidity, it may be observed that merely one kind of experience, sufficiently realized, will suffice for an almost unlimited progression of imaginative analogies: the one experience will be ballast enough to carry the author through any fictive evocation of feelings and actions. The case of Dostoevsky is very illustrative of this truth; and the life of Charlotte Brontë is well worth consideration precisely because the process, the logic, is there seen so uncontaminated by subsidiary influences.

Experience alone does not, of course, make the poet or novelist; it merely qualifies him. It must be united with a previous disposition to create an imaginary world, the origin of which, as I have suggested, is to be found in psychological factors at work during infancy and adolescence. Charlotte early had " the desire (almost amounting to illness) of expressing herself in some way,—writing or drawing ".[1] At school she developed a talent, under the guise of play, of " making things out ". " This habit ", one of her school friends relates, " of 'making out' interests for themselves that most children get who have none in actual life, was very strong in her. The whole family used to 'make out' histories, and invent characters and events. I told her sometimes they were like growing potatoes in a cellar. She said, sadly, 'Yes! I know we are!' " The greater bulk of the unpublished Brontë manuscripts seems to consist of an elaborate " cycle " of stories and poems, written over a long period of years and concerned with the politics and chivalry of a kingdom imagined in every detail. To revert to the old antithesis, these were works of idle fancy; but when bleak disillusionment was added to the already sufficiently bleak existence of these children, when expression became a more serious necessity as an escape from emotional agitations too strong to be repressed with impunity, then the mere mechanism of literary expression was ready at their command.

This is to put the matter on its deterministic level; it is perhaps of more profit to note the

[1] Mrs. Gaskell's account of conversations with Charlotte. See *Life*, chap. xxvii.

conscious reactions of Charlotte to these emotional and mental transitions. There are two points to notice: her theory of the relation of experience to imagination; and the evolution, at her hands, of the analytic method in fiction. The best expression of the first point was elicited during Charlotte's brief correspondence with G. H. Lewes—a literary encounter very peculiar to the period and about which an effect of exquisite comedy lurks. On 6th November 1847 she wrote in reply to a friendly letter of Lewes's, dictated by his enthusiasm for *Jane Eyre*: "You advise me, too, not to stray far from the ground of experience, as I become weak when I enter the region of fiction, and you say, 'real experience is perennially interesting, and to all men'. I feel that this is also true; but, dear sir, is not the real experience of each individual very limited? And if a writer dwells upon that solely or principally, is he not in danger of repeating himself, and also of becoming an egotist? Then, too, imagination is a strong, restless faculty, which claims to be heard and exercised: are we to be quite deaf to her cry, and insensate to her struggles? When she shows us bright pictures, are we never to look at them, and try to reproduce them? And when she is eloquent, and speaks rapidly and urgently in our ear, are we not to write to her dictation?"

In reading this passage we must remember that Charlotte writes conscious of what she could but regard as a salutary lesson in the strategy of authorship: this was the complete failure of her first novel, *The Professor*, in which, as Mrs. Gaskell says, " she went to the extreme of reality, depicting characters as they had shown themselves to her in actual life ". And in the letter to Lewes already quoted, Charlotte herself confessed: " When I first began to write, so impressed was I with the truth of the principles you advocate, that I determined to take Nature and Truth as my sole guides, and to follow their very footprints; I restrained imagination, eschewed romance, repressed excitement; over-bright colouring, too, I avoided, and sought to produce something which should be soft, grave, and true." But the publishers would have none of it, and the convenient theory of art for art's sake not being yet a part of the literary consciousness, she had decided to modify her virtuous course. She abandoned the mere transcript of experience and adopted the imaginative process I have tried to define.[1] It is here that we must realize the essential strength of her character

[1] It is interesting to note her own subsequent and detached opinion of the qualities which, nevertheless, did result from her first method. In a letter to W. S. Williams dated 14th December 1847, she writes: " A few days since I looked over *The Professor*. I found the beginning very feeble, the whole narrative deficient in incident and in general attractiveness. Yet the middle and latter portion of the work, all that relates to Brussels, the Belgian school, etc., is as good as I can write; it contains more pith, more substance, more reality, in my judgment, than much of *Jane Eyre*. It gives, I think, a new view of a grade, an occupation, and a class of characters—all

and genius: a weaker writer would have had recourse to the less intense forms of imaginative activity; but Charlotte, driven, perhaps, by subconscious forces, determined, in her own phrase, to be " her own woman ". She determined to see justly rather than to feel kindly; and when she was almost agonized by the suggestion, emanating from the *Quarterly*, but eagerly repeated even by the kind of people she herself thought nice, that *Jane Eyre* was a " wicked book ", even then she had the courage of her magnificent retort: " I am resolved not to write otherwise. *I shall bend as my powers tend.*"

Her powers resided in her intuitive logic, though she rather tended to mask the incidence of her faculty. " We only suffer reality to *suggest*, never to *dictate*," she writes to her old school friend; and some years later, with *Villette* fresh from her pen, she even went so far as to enunciate this slightly insincere maxim: " I hold that a work of fiction ought to be a work of creation: that the *real* should be sparingly introduced in pages dedicated to the *ideal*." This hardly tallies with her own criticism of *Villette*: " I greatly apprehend that the weakest character in the book is the one I aimed at making the most beautiful; and, if this be the case, the fault lies in its wanting the germ of the *real*—in its being purely imaginary."

very commonplace, very insignificant in themselves, but not more so than the materials composing that portion of *Jane Eyre* which seems to please most generally."

We have in this latter statement, self-analysed and self-confessed, the whole secret of her strength. Her practice of fiction resolves always into a nucleus of experience and the growth, from this nucleus, of an imaginative organism "given off", as in nature, cell by cell, with inexorable continuity.

Combined with this process, a part of its mechanism, was the gift of analysis. Some years before she began to write, even before her education at Brussels, she was aware of her capabilities in this direction. She warned a rejected suitor, who wished to become her "friend", that "it has always been my habit to study the character of those amongst whom I chance to be thrown. . . . As for me, you do not know me: I am not the serious, grave, cool-headed individual you would suppose: you would think me romantic and eccentric; you would say I was satirical and severe." The two faculties of her writing are clearly foreshadowed here: imagination and analysis. There is no need to enlarge upon this second quality; it is so obviously her distinction. The consistency of its exercise—as, for example, in the character of Madame Beck—is perhaps for her date a matter for wonder. She herself remarks of Balzac: "By-and-by I seemed to enter into the mystery of his craft, and to discover, with delight, where his force lay: is it not in the analysis of motive, and in a subtle perception of the most obscure and secret workings of the mind?" But at the time of her first introduction to Balzac's work, her own gift was already fully formed. I find no evidence anywhere that she knew the work of Stendhal, or the solitary masterpiece of Benjamin Constant; but she introduced into English literature the very qualities of psychological observation and analysis by which these writers had instituted a new epoch in the literature of France.

The influence she exercised on the development of the English novel was more profound than is often acknowledged: it is *Villette*, more than any work of Thackeray or George Eliot, that we must recognize as the pioneer of an extension of the province and function of the novelist's art only completely worked into the tradition of the English novel by Meredith and Henry James. To her contemporaries this revolutionary element in her work was quite evident, and though they did not stop to consider its real nature, they disliked it strongly because it was strange. Open-minded critics of the stamp of Lewes and Thackeray were willing to acknowledge the power and originality of her art, but the more average minds of the time experienced a sense of shock, deepening to outrage when it gradually became evident that the mysterious Currer Bell belonged to the gentler sex. The particular charge, first raised against *Jane Eyre*, but repeated in the case of *Shirley*, was one of " coarseness ". What her accusers meant by their term cannot be very vivid to our modern consciousness: all they meant would, I think, easily be included in our concept "realism". But even Mrs. Gaskell, who by no means shared all the prudery of her age, thought it necessary to apologize for this lapse on the part of her heroine; and did so in these curious sentences:

"I do not deny for myself the existence of coarseness here and there in her works, otherwise so entirely noble. I only ask those who read them to consider her life,—which has been openly laid bare before them,—and to say how it could be otherwise. She saw few men; and among these few were one or two with whom she had been acquainted since early childhood,—who had shown her much friendliness and kindness,—through whose family she had received many pleasures,—for whose intellect she had a great respect,—but who talked before her, if not to her, with as little reticence as Rochester talked to Jane Eyre. Take this in connection with her poor brother's sad life, and the outspoken people among whom she lived, —remember her strong feeling of the duty of representing life as it really is, not as it ought to be,—and then do her justice for all that she was, and all that she would have been (had God spared her), rather than censure her because circumstances forced her to touch pitch, as it were, and by it her hand was for a moment defiled" (*Life*, chap. xxvi).

Charlotte herself could not comprehend the charge; and her unconsciousness of the very existence of what her critics so plainly realized, brings before us in all its uniqueness the amazing quality of *innocence* which distinguishes, not only her own work, but that of her sisters also. It is because the art was so innocent that it is so real. One can only account for the phenomenon by the unparalleled isolation of their lives. Though from an early age they devoured every scrap of literature that came within their reach, it is doubtful if anything of a directly inspiring kind ever came their way before Charlotte's and Emily's departure for Brussels. At Haworth they seem to have been confined to a diet of newspapers, sermons, and the Bible; and at Brussels, though in the matter of style and composition their reading there had incalculable influence, yet it seems certain that, with the possible exception of Hoffmann and Rousseau, it did not include anything that could form a model for their own efforts. At any rate, whatever the explanation, it is certain that when the three sisters solemnly and in unison sat down to compose their first serious novels, they did so without any prepossessions. They are the least influenced and most original geniuses in the whole history of the English novel. And what Charlotte in her Introduction to *Wuthering Heights* wrote of the others, was equally true of herself: "Neither Ellis nor Acton was learned: they had no thoughts of filling their pitchers at the well-spring of other minds; they always wrote from the impulse of nature, the dictates of intuition, and from such stores of observation as their limited experience had enabled them to amass."

It is this quality of innocence that gives to *Wuthering Heights* its terrible and unique intensity. If I have written of Charlotte to the neglect of Emily, it is not that for one moment I make the mistake of attaching more importance to her. It is merely that in the case of Charlotte the evidence is so much more ample. The psychology of Emily is at once less complex and more profoundly hidden. She is one of the strangest geniuses in our literature, and her kinship is with Baudelaire and Poe. It is not merely that her imagination traverses the same sombre shadows, but also like these two anguished minds, she is forever perplexed by the problem of evil—"conquered good and conquering ill". Her absorption in metaphysical problems has no parallel in the poetry of her age, and in her "Last Lines" rises to an intensity of emotional thought not surpassed in the whole range of English literature. Yet this same mind was capable of the purest lyrical utterance—in which, however, the sense of mortality seems to linger:

> Fall, leaves, fall; die, flowers, away;
> Lengthen night, and shorten day!
> Every leaf speaks bliss to me,
> Fluttering from the autumn tree.
>
> I shall smile when wreaths of snow
> Blossom where the rose should grow;
> I shall sing when night's decay
> Ushers in a drearier day.

Emily Brontë's poetry, which is at once explicit

and profound, with sense finely annealed to cadence, is the most essential poetry ever written by a woman in the English tongue. Her mind, far more daring than Charlotte's, soared above particular creeds and attained in a few momentary manifestations those universal forms of thought common only to minds of the first order. Her best poems suffer, at present, by being bound up with much that is juvenile and occasional in kind. *Wuthering Heights* remains, the towering rock of Charlotte's metaphor, extremely definite, completely achieved, and of an amazing unity of tone.

We are left with one other element, common to Emily and Charlotte, which needs a word of notice. A certain lack of reticence had shocked the ruck of their Victorian critics; a smaller and a rarer band were disturbed by the evident rapture. It fell to Harriet Martineau, economist, moralist, agnostic, and a very typical representative of her age, to bring this criticism to a head. Despite a friendship she had formed for Charlotte, she had felt bound to air her misgivings in *The Daily News*, and in a review of *Villette* had insisted that Charlotte made love too general and too absorbing a factor in women's lives, protesting against the assumption that " events and characters are to be regarded through the medium of one passion only ". Charlotte demurred, but Miss Martineau, indomitable and pitiless, wrote to her: " I do not like the love, either the kind or the degree of it; and its prevalence in the book and effect on the action of it, help to explain the passages in the reviews which you consulted me about, and seem to afford *some* foundation for the criticisms they offered." Charlotte retired abashed; she had but followed " the impulses of nature and the dictates of intuition ". And about this very book she had written to her publisher: " Unless I am mistaken, the emotion of the book will be found to be kept throughout in tolerable subjection." Emotion in subjection—that is the very definition of art! And because Miss Martineau did not realize this, she has become a curious paleolithic dummy, an Aunt Sally ready for our modern ironists, whilst Charlotte still lives in her books with all the directness of a real personality.

But it is not Miss Martineau that was destined to stand as the antitype to the Brontës: a subtler and finer antagonist had been in the field for some time. It speaks a good deal for Charlotte's critical perception that she realized the implications of Miss Austen's talent as soon as she became aware of it, rather late in her life, and, though only in the privacy of her correspondence with her publisher, she then defined the limitations of that talent in terms which still remain unanswerable. In a letter written in 1850 she says: " She does her business of delineating the surface of the lives of genteel English people curiously well. There is a Chinese fidelity, a miniature delicacy in the painting. She ruffles her reader by nothing vehement, disturbs him by nothing profound. The passions are perfectly unknown to her; she rejects even a speaking acquaintance with that stormy sisterhood. Even to the feelings she vouchsafes no more than an occasional graceful but distant recognition—too frequent converse with them would ruffle the smooth elegance of her progress. Her business is not half so much with the human heart as with the human eyes, mouth, hands, and feet. What sees keenly, speaks aptly, moves flexibly, it suits her to study; but what throbs fast and full, though hidden, what the blood rushes through, what is the unseen seat of life and the sentient target of death—this Miss Austen ignores." The justice of that analysis remains, to confront the present sophisticated rage for Jane Austen. But it also remains the statement of an extreme position, the weakness of which would have been exceedingly patent to the precise sensibility of the author of *Pride and Prejudice*. If she had lived long enough she might have criticized *Jane Eyre* in terms almost exactly contranominal to those of Charlotte. The psychologist does not venture to take sides in such an opposition, but resorts to his theory of types, and sees here the dry bones of his structure take on perfect flesh. It would be difficult to discover a more exact illustration of the main distinction he draws between faculties directed inwards, to the observation of feeling, and faculties directed outwards, to the observation of external things. The psychologist must halt at this distinction, unless he suggests, as a scientific ideal, some harmony or balance of these tendencies. But the critic must pursue the matter to a judgement. It will not, for that purpose, suffice to identify the ordered conception of objective facts with the classical spirit, or the research of passion with the romantic spirit—though it is tempting in this case to think of Jane Austen as a typical (though rare, because feminine) embodiment of classicism, and Pater seized on *Wuthering Heights*, in preference to any work of Scott's, as the " really characteristic fruit " of the spirit of romanticism. That only proves once more the inadequacy of these outworn shibboleths, since from another point of view *Wuthering Heights*, with its unerring unity of conception and its full catharsis of the emotions of pity and terror, is one of the very few occasions on which the novel has reached the dignity of classical tragedy. And, in the other case, it would be hard to concede the full meaning of classicism to Jane Austen's universe of undertones.

We return to Charlotte's phrase—emotion in subjection—and contend that this is the only normal sense in which the classical spirit should be endured. The rest is pedantry, academic closures, and the " literature of our grandfathers ". To apply the distinction to Jane Austen is hardly fair: she belongs to the spirit of comedy, which has never been easily classified, always existing as a free and detached criticism of life and literature. Jane Austen, in essentials, takes her place with Congreve, if with anybody in English letters;

and maybe, after all, in making her the antitype to the Brontës we are but displaying the old discordant masks side by side. Is it an equal opposition? Well, not quite. Charlotte Brontë is again the critic—" Miss Austen being, as you say, without 'sentiment', without *poetry*, maybe *is* sensible, real (more *real* than *true*), but she cannot be great." And that might be said equally well of Congreve, or of any representative of the comic spirit. It is a question of attitude. It is, finally, a question of courage—of throwing into the attempt for truth not only intelligence, spirit, faith, but also feeling, emotion, self.

X

TOBIAS SMOLLETT

It has long been a commonplace of criticism that Smollett is the most neglected of our eighteenth-century authors, and it may be that the gradual emergence of a freer sensibility in manners and literature makes it possible for us to redress our judgements. It is not a question of recovering from the reaction of a generation that has grown tired of the habit of praise; nor is there the excuse of original obscurity, as in the case of Blake or Melville. We have rather a series of carelessly propagated *clichés*, derived perhaps from Sir Walter Scott, and given general critical currency by Hazlitt and Thackeray; and these *clichés*, not carrying conviction, are disregarded. The traditional view of the man and his work takes two parallel courses—it expatiates on his humour and deprecates his indecency. But the truth is that Smollett was not essentially a humorist, and that the charge of indecency is, if not meaningless, at least misleading.

The early conditions of Smollett's life were such as to induce a spirit of self-reliance in a temperament of sensibility and pride. He was left without a father while still an infant, and though his relations were in fair enough circumstances to give him a good education, they did not consult his wishes to the extent of his ambitions; and at the age of fifteen he found himself apprenticed to a surgeon, but without any real enthusiasm for that calling. His interest tended rather to literature and the humanities, though this interest, we can see, was not of the tender-minded sort. That is to say, Smollett did not seek intellectual accomplishments as a compensation for physical deficiencies, but, like Goethe, is a precious witness to the possible normality of genius.

He left Glasgow at the age of eighteen and made his way to London, fully confident that a tragedy he had written, *The Regicide*, would be an Open Sesame to fame and fortune. This play is a wretched affair, pompous, insipid, and at times positively ludicrous. It has neither poetry nor wit; and it is astonishing that anyone of Smollett's practical temperament could have made it the occasion for so much resentment and false pride. He was incensed at his failure to provoke the least interest in his production and at his wit's end for a living. He finally secured a position as surgeon's mate in the Navy, and in this capacity he took part in the war against Spain. Of this experience he has left us an account, not only in *Roderick Random*, but also in a characteristic but neglected narrative called "The Expedition against Carthagena." This was first published in 1756 in Smollett's *Compendium of Authentic and Entertaining Voyages*, and though not of any great length is distinguished by its direct realism and fearless censure. A passage like the following shows that warfare in the eighteenth century had horrors to equal the scientific barbarisms of our more antiseptic age:

"As for the sick and wounded, they were next day sent on board of the transports and vessels called hospital-ships, where they languished in want of every necessary comfort and accommodation. They were destitute of surgeons, nurses, cooks, and proper provision; they were pent up between decks in small vessels where they had not room to sit upright; they wallowed in filth; myriads of maggots were hatched in the putrefaction of their sores, which had no other dressing than that of being washed by themselves with their own allowance of brandy; and nothing was heard but groans, lamentations, and the language of despair invoking death to deliver them from their miseries. What served to encourage this despondency was the prospect of those poor wretches who had strength and opportunity to look around them; for there they beheld the naked bodies of their fellow-soldiers and comrades floating up and down the harbour, affording prey to the carrion crows and sharks, which tore them in pieces without interruption, and contributed by their stench to the mortality that prevailed."

Smollett left the Fleet at Jamaica; and there he seems to have stayed two or three years, in the society of a congenial Scotch colony. And while there he fell in love with the daughter of a planter, Nancy Lascelles, and to her he was married on his return to London. It is a curious but undeniable fact that this author whose books have for a century or more been surrounded with an aura of infamy, and whose very name was mentioned only in the smoking-room, lived all his life a faithful husband and devoted father. Upon his return from the West Indies he set up a practice as surgeon in Downing Street; but he is said to have lacked an agreeable bedside manner, and in any case he was no success in the profession. He was still intent on literary fame—still confident, in fact, of the merits of *The Regicide*. But in the hands of Richardson and Fielding the novel was just at that time in the ascendancy, and Smollett resolved to try his fortune with this form. The result was *Roderick Random*. Its success was immediate, and Smollett from that moment determined to make his living by his pen.

We need not follow any further the immediate course of his career, but should rather pause to take stock of the qualities he had exhibited in his first novel. We may in the first place dissociate his work almost entirely from Fielding's. *Joseph Andrews* was perhaps an economic cause of Smollett's work, but it had nothing to do with its internal inspiration. For that it had nearer sponsors in Defoe and Le Sage. And though in general we cannot claim for Smollett anything like the profound humanism of Fielding, yet in point of style Smollett, as Hazlitt acknowledged, was the better man. In this particular he was more allied to Swift, and cultivated a clean impersonal mode, devoid of mannerisms. His sentences flow with the even rhythm of economy and ease. For incidents (we can scarcely speak of plot) he relied mainly on his experiences, and the imagination he expends on these is mainly visual. His mind is innocent of ideas, and indeed of abstractions of any sort, and he is at the best but an arranger of the objective facts of existence. Such an imagination is not necessarily of an inferior order, and indeed may achieve a clarity hardly possible to imaginations of a more intuitive or speculative order. Smollett never indulges in introspection of any sort, and the only subjective feeling he ever gives the rein to is the *saeva indignatio* of the satirist—too often, in his case, a mere reaction to the peevish nature of his constitution (the *systema nervosum maxime irritabile* of his own diagnosis).

Roderick Random certainly determined Smollett's career, but it does not reveal, any more than *Peregrine Pickle* or *Humphry Clinker*, the true quality of his talent. Smollett's was a logical and sequestered mind; and of the two strains—rationality and artificiality—whose inter-play makes for the peculiar complexity of the eighteenth century, he at least was an unconfused exponent of reason. *Roderick Random* was published in 1748; *Peregrine Pickle* and *Ferdinand*, *Count Fathom* followed fairly quickly, in 1751 and 1753. There then ensued a period of seventeen years during which Smollett produced no fiction, with the exception of *Sir Launcelot Greaves*, a *feuilleton* of the most haphazard origin. But these seventeen years were years of the most unremitting literary labour, and to omit to reckon them in any estimate of Smollett is as though we were to ignore in Milton's case the twenty years that elapsed between *Lycidas* and *Paradise Lost*. In that interval Smollett translated *Don Quixote*, edited a famous literary review, wrote a *History of England* in four quarto volumes, brought out a farce, edited the *Compendium of Voyages* already mentioned (a work in seven volumes), organized and partly wrote a " universal history ", revised his history of England and published it in sixpenny weekly parts, was imprisoned for libel, carried on a second magazine, edited a translation of the complete works of Voltaire in thirty-eight volumes, published a *Continuation of the History of England* (five volumes), as well as a work entitled *The Present State of All Nations*, a geographical compendium in eight large volumes. Finally, he threw himself into political journalism as a champion of Bute's administration; and this last venture led to a breach with Wilkes, a politician he really admired. Worn out with vexations of every kind, his health ruined by the long sedentary labours he had undergone, he was already a broken man when the death of his only daughter in 1763 came as a final blow and compelled him to resign everything and go abroad in search of life itself.

We have as a record of this journey the *Travels through France and Italy*—certainly the most important source of our understanding of the man Smollett. His temperament as there revealed is mainly a compost of superficial irascibility and fundamental good nature—the *bourru bienfaisant* of Austin Dobson's phrase. But what is of more interest is the revelation of Smollett's mind—its independence, its complete freedom from the second-hand claptrap that almost every traveller repeats from his guide-book, and its complete disregard for the fashionable and dilettante opinions of his contemporaries. This frankness is best expressed in his aesthetic judgements, and these have been the laughing-stock of the world ever since Sterne made fun of them in the famous passage about Smelfungus. How many readers of Sterne's ridicule of Smollett, particularly of his judgement of the Venus de' Medici, have ever cared to refer to the original, and to consider Smollett's actual words? Sterne's is a good joke, not to be denied at any cost; but is Smollett so absurd after all?

"With respect to the famous Venus Pontia, commonly called *de Medicis*, which was found at Tivoli, and is kept in a separate apartment called the *Tribuna*, I believe I ought to be intirely silent, or at least conceal my real sentiments, which will otherwise appear equally absurd and presumptuous. It must be want of taste that prevents my feeling that enthusiastic admiration with which others are inspired at sight of this statue; a statue which in reputation equals that of Cupid by Praxiteles, which brought such a concourse of strangers of old to the little town of Thespiae. I cannot help thinking that there is no beauty in the features of Venus; and that the attitude is awkward and out of character. It is a bad plea to urge that the antients and we differ in the ideas of beauty. We know the contrary, from their medals, busts, and historians. Without all doubt, the limbs and proportions of this statue are elegantly formed, and accurately designed, according to the nicest rules of symmetry and proportion; and the back parts especially are executed so happily as to excite the admiration of the most indifferent spectator."

Smollett, it will be seen, moves heavily in this unfamiliar ground of aesthetic appreciation; but there is an honest attempt to come to terms with truth, and it may be doubted whether any modern traveller of average sensibility would express himself with an equal disregard for " the ridicule of the virtuosi ". This, too, can be said for Smollett: he was aware of the limitations of common sense; elsewhere in his *Travels* he writes: " I am used to speak my mind freely on all subjects that fall under the cognizance of my senses; though I must as freely own, there is something more than common sense required to discover and distinguish the more delicate beauties of painting." His mind, of course, was not quite free; it was under the dominion of those classical prejudices which make most eighteenth-century aesthetic criticism intemperate. But within his limits Smollett shows a good deal of penetration. At Pisa he was charmed with " the brass gates, designed and executed by John of Bologna, representing, embossed in different compartments, the history of the Old and New Testament. I was so charmed with this work that I could have stood a whole day to examine and admire it ". And when he got to Florence, in front of Ghiberti's doors, he " still retained a greater veneration for those at Pisa—a preference which either arises from want of taste, or from the charm of novelty, by which the former were recommended to my attention ". If Smollett were to revisit the scene to-day, he might find even certain of the virtuosi sharing his want of taste! His remarks on Giotto are intelligent for his time, and in this judgement of a "basso-relievo " he saw in the Campo Santo at Pisa there is a freshness worth many of the expansive similes of less phlegmatic travellers:

" I was struck with the figure of a woman lying dead on a tombstone, covered with a piece of thin drapery, so delicately cut as to show all the flexures of the attitude, and even all the swellings and sinuosities of the muscles. Instead of stone, it looks like a sheet of wet linen."

His criticism of Michel Angelo's Pietà at St. Peter's is surprising in an author of his reputation: he found " something indelicate, not to say indecent, in the attitude and design of a man's body, stark naked, lying upon the knees of a woman"; and before the "Last Judgment" in the Sistine Chapel he uttered this remark, which has more acuteness in it:

"Michel Angelo, with all his skill in anatomy, his correctness of design, his grand composition, his fire, and force of expression, seems to have had very little idea of grace."

It was necessary to expatiate a little on these aesthetic judgements of Smollett's because they show a side of his mind in sharp contrast with the ordinary conception of his personality. Of the same tendency are his views on religion, which are rationalistic (he compared Catholicism and Calvinism to the comic and tragic masks of the human drama); his serious antiquarianism (he measured the arena of the amphitheatre at Cemenelum with packthread); and his curious philological digressions, introduced on the least provocation.

But we must now turn to consider the nature of Smollett's humour, which is, when all is said and done, the true basis of his claim on modern readers. We use the word "humour" without any hesitation, for no one ever accused Smollett of wit. The distinction between wit and humour is one of the favourite exercises of philosophical critics and serious psychologists; but perhaps Hazlitt's distinction, having our immediate subject-matter in mind, is most apt:

"Humour is the describing the ludicrous as it is in itself; wit is the exposing it, by comparing or contrasting it with something else. Humour is, as it were, the growth of nature and accident; wit is the product of art and fancy. Humour, as it is shewn in books, is an imitation of the natural or acquired absurdities of mankind, of the ludicrous in accident, situation, and character; wit is the illustrating and heightening the sense of that absurdity by some sudden and unexpected likeness or opposition of one thing to another, which sets off the quality we laugh at or despise in a still more contemptible or striking point of view."

We may add a modern *nuance* to these distinctions by showing how well they fit in with those distinctions in the human personality elaborated by modern psychology. Humour is descriptive, external, accidental, imitative—that is, an objective faculty. Wit is introspective, comparative, analytical—that is, a subjective faculty. And the exercise of these faculties is appropriate to temperaments that correspond—to the objective man, or extravert, in the one case; to the subjective man, or introvert, in the other case. Now Smollett, as we have seen, was essentially an extravert; and his mind, full of the observation of events rather than the consideration of ideas, naturally expressed itself in terms of humour rather than of wit.

The originality of Smollett's humour lay not so much in its character as in the mode of employment. He took over a form of prose fiction established by Le Sage and Scarron, and introduced it to English literature; he infused it with a certain element of humour which we like to consider distinctively English, and which we trace to Shakespeare. As a matter of fact, Smollett is, for an eighteenth-century writer, oddly conversant with Shakespeare; *Count Fathom* especially is sprinkled with quotations from the plays. It seems that he takes a certain element direct from Shakespeare—the element of Falstaff and Bardolph—and extends it with his peculiar talent for imaginative extension. The words that greeted Fathom as he entered the " mansions of misery " are very Elizabethan:

" You, Bess Beetle, score a couple of fresh eggs, a pennyworth of butter, and half a pint of mountain to the king; and stop credit till the bill is paid: he is now debtor for fifteen shillings and sixpence, and damn me if I trust him one farthing more, if he was the best king in Christendom; and d'ye hear, send Ragged-head with five pounds of potatoes for Major Macleaver's supper, and let him have what drink he wants; the fat widow gentlewoman from Pimlico has promised to quit his score. Sir Mungo Barebones may have some hasty pudding and small beer, though I don't expect to see his coin, no more than to receive the eighteen pence I laid out for a pair of breeches to his backside—what then? He's a quiet sort of body and a great scholar, and it was a scandal to see him going about in that naked condition."

But Commodore Trunnion's ride to church, and the entertainment in the manner of the ancients, in *Peregrine Pickle*, are something more. We pass from realism to phantasy, and the phantasy is, as Hazlitt objected, rather vulgar. Someone in the character of clown has entered the arena of literature, and the fun is never quite the same thereafter. Though we are diverted well enough on the first occasion—which may well be in Smollett—we are appalled to think of the progeny. Many of us might prefer to come first to Mr. Pickwick or Mr. Jorrocks, instead of Commodore Trunnion and Lieutenant Lismahago, and so get our vulgarity neat. But in the mass these humorists fairly break away with the English reputation for wit. How could we answer a charge that we have seen in this array of grotesques a sufficient apology for our want of intelligence and subtlety? In our right senses we cling more desperately to Sterne. He had few of the civic virtues of Smollett, but his grace was a guardian angel for all occasions. Sterne, indeed, is the right foil for Smollett; bring these two in opposition and all the richest lights and colours emerge on each in admirable contrast. But then Sterne is incomparable. Goethe called him the freest spirit of his century; and Nietzsche, in the profoundest criticism ever written of Sterne,[1] took up Goethe's words and called him the freest writer of all time.

" Compared with him all other writers are stiff, clumsy, intolerant and absolutely boorish. He is

[1] *Menschliches, Allzumenschliches*, vol. ii ("Vermischte Meinungen und Sprüche", Aph. 113, Der freiste Schriftsteller).

to be praised, not for his clear, finished form, but for his 'infinite melody'—if by such a phrase we can give a name to a style in art where the selected form is continually broken, disregarded, thrust back into the indeterminate, so that it signifies one thing and at the same time another thing."

And Nietzsche then applies to Sterne one of those epithets which serve for all time, and calls him "der grosse Meister der Zweideutigkeit", a phrase for which there is no precise English equivalent.

Midway between Sterne and Smollett is Diderot. The bare recital of Smollett's professional activities will have suggested a comparison with the great "father of the encyclopaedia"; and in their rational temperaments these authors had much in common, though Diderot's was a more inquiring mind, and a mind, of course, much more introspective and philosophical. But in the superficial aspect of their careers these two correspond; and there is even a possibility that the author of *Le Neveu de Rameau* and *Jacques le Fataliste* owed something to the author of *Roderick Random* and *Peregrine Pickle*. But perhaps he owed more to the author of *Tristram Shandy*; for the French, as Nietzsche observes, are too serious for humour—above all, for this humoristic fashion of exploiting humour. Smollett's humour, however, was not all pure buffoonery, and he himself at any rate would have maintained that it was inspired by a satirical intention. That intention could, if need be, blaze out without any equivocation whatsoever; and *The Adventures of an Atom* is too savage for most people's taste. It is even too much for the sober critic, who sees in satire something closely bound to the real. Once it transcends the real it enters another category—that of humour in Smollett's case. His caricatures of humanity—Uncle Bowling, Strap, Peregrine, Trunnion, Fathom, Tabitha, and the rest—are too extravagant to affect the conscience of a public; yet that is the function of satire. We immediately feel that we ourselves live in a different world, less fantastic, less amusing. We do not have the same agreeable illusion about the Yahoos.

Finally, there is the question of indecency. Smollett himself, in the first chapter of *Count Fathom*, was at some pains to defend himself against this charge:

" Have a little patience, gentle, delicate, sublime critic; you, I doubt not, are one of those consummate connoisseurs, who, in their purifications, let humour evaporate, while they endeavour to preserve decorum, and polish wit, until the edge of it is quite wore off; or, perhaps, of that class, who, in the sapience of taste, are disgusted with those very flavours in the productions of their own country, which have yielded infinite delectation to their faculties, when imported from another clime; and damn an author in despite of all precedent and prescription—who extol the writings of Petronius Arbiter, read with rapture the amorous sallies of Ovid's pen, and chuckle over the story of Lucian's ass; yet, if a modern author presumes to relate the progress of a simple intrigue, are shocked at the indecency and immorality of the scene—who delight in following Guzman d'Alfarache through all the mazes of squalid beggary; who with pleasure accompany Don Quixote and his squire, in the lowest paths of fortune; who are diverted with the adventures of Scarron's ragged troop of strollers, and highly entertained with the servile situations of Gil Blas; yet, when a character in humble life occasionally occurs in a performance of our own growth, exclaim, with an air of disgust, 'Was ever anything so mean! sure, this writer must have been very conversant with the lowest scenes of life'; who, when Swift or Pope represents a coxcomb in the act of swearing, scruple not to laugh at the ridiculous execrations; but, in a less reputed author, condemn the use of such profane expletives; who eagerly explore the jakes of Rabelais for amusement, and even extract humour from the dean's description of a lady's dressing-room; yet, in a production of these days, unstamped with such venerable names, will stop their noses, with all the signs of loathing and abhorrence, at a bare mention of the china chamber-pot; who applaud Catullus, Juvenal, Persius, and Lucan, for their spirit in lashing the greatest names of antiquity; yet, when a British satirist, of this generation, has courage enough to call in question the talents of a pseudo-patron in power, accuse him of insolence, rancour, and scurrility."

That defence may still speak for itself; and though, like Smollett, we must refrain from discussing the ethics of the question, we might at least make one or two distinctions which are of its essence. Indecency is of many sorts; and though we need not extenuate the ethical condemnation of any of them, we must insist that there is a scale of values in this as in all other matters of conduct. Distinct words, like obscenity, eroticism, blasphemy, pornography, and coprology (or scatology) do not exist without a purpose; but this subject is so often treated with a lack of frankness that their connotation is always uncertain, and a writer like Smollett is in danger of having any or all of these opprobrious terms heaped upon him without discrimination. As a matter of fact, Smollett is never obscene or blasphemous, nor in any but a limited sense pornographical or erotic. The "Memoirs of a Lady of Quality" in *Peregrine Pickle*, which Robert Chambers described in his biography of Smollett as "a recital which could not show face in any decent company" (and perhaps for that reason he always refers to them as the "Memoirs of a *Woman* of Quality") is, nevertheless, a recital absolutely free from the sensuality that would inevitably distinguish such a narrative in modern hands. Smollett is not sensual; it is almost our complaint that he is not sensual enough. In short, his indiscretions are confined to the coprological kind: that is to say, they hover round certain daily physical acts to which we are all subject, but of which only the neurotic are ashamed. It may be that such acts are not a proper subject for humour; but humour being by definition an imitation of the ludicrous in nature, and nothing being more ludicrous than a dignified human being's submission to these necessities, it is difficult to escape from, at any rate, a logical defence of coprological humour. It may be objected, however, that realism is not of the essence of indecency, but that everything is determined by the manner of it. There is every difference, for example, between the plain realism of Rabelais's coprology and the subjective disgust of Mr. Joyce's. There is also every difference between the matter-of-fact narrative of Smollett and the equivocal suggestions of Sterne. But this all redounds to the credit of Smollett: he is everywhere masculine and healthy, direct and unfurtive. *Humphry Clinker* is the epitome of all these qualities. This admirable book came in the twilight of Smollett's life—he only just lived to see its appearance—and it has a serenity and harmony fitting to the time of its origin. The humour is quieter, the pace is unforced; there is no pretence of plot, no unction of satirical purpose, but, as Professor Saintsbury once noted, " an almost Shakespearean touch of sureness, completeness, self-sufficingness ". Matt Bramble is the centre of this unflurried stage; and Matt Bramble is Smollett himself, mellow, loquacious, quizzically surveying at a distance the manners and economy of his native land. And at bottom the work is still serious; the book is rational despite its immense fund of humour; for all its types and oddities are ranged like puppets against a clean curtain of common sense. In this manner Smollett took his leave of a scene where he had lived dangerously and met defeat—but a defeat of the body, not of the spirit. He once anonymously described himself as " one of those few writers of the age that stand upon their own foundation, without patronage, and above dependence ". There are few self-opinions that posterity can so agreeably confirm.

XI

THE MODERN NOVEL

(Cursory Notes)

Action. HISTORICALLY, the many tributaries of the novel seem to gather into two main streams, which we can imagine as the novel descriptive of action and the novel descriptive of temperamental relationships. As an effect of the Romantic Movement, the former stream was dammed, or robbed at its sources, or otherwise deviated, and the modern development has been almost entirely along the stream of temperamental relationships. It is worth considering whether we may have come to the end of that development. A tremendous expansion of intelligent consciousness has been achieved, but possibly all that was to be achieved by this particular method has been done, and after Flaubert and Proust there can be little more than an etiolation of the finished product. Meanwhile there is a wilful neglect of the more masculine force—the epic poem, the epic drama, and the novel of action.

The essential of an epic is that it should embody some corporate spirit, revealing actions as determined to some end, and sanctioning, by the human value of that end, the bleak energy of the narrated events. And so Conrad cannot be claimed as an epic novelist. He does not idealize the heroic, or make it more than the expression of an individual temperament. There is a certain limited scope for Conrad's art: it has advanced a little, and that laterally, from the main stream. It incorporates certain new strands of experience. But in the end it merely lifts the veil from one more alcove of temperamental privacy.

Duration. Some time ago, when reviewing Monsieur Abel Chevalley's *Le Roman Anglais de Notre Temps* for *La Nouvelle Revue Française*, Monsieur Thibaudet ventured to question the whole Flaubertian tradition, and to throw doubt upon the fastidious search for a perfect form. He began by distinguishing between the meaning of the word " composition " as applied to the novel and to the drama. Dramatic form, with its unities, its " situations ", is a composition in space rather than in time. It is a geometrical symmetry rather than a rhythm. But the novel, "le roman-nature ", reflects immediacy; it is life itself in flux and duration. It is not " composed " because composition only exists where there is concentration, or, in the extreme case, simultaneity, in space. Or, as it might be said, a novel is not *composed*: it is disposed. It is not the result of an idea: it is itself a fund of ideas. In short, the most that can be said is that there may be evidence of a certain form after the novel has been written, but such form did not exist as a preconceived idea in the mind of the novelist before he put pen to paper.

There is something very attractive about this theory for the simple reason that it so beautifully fits certain facts. No one, I think, wishes to question the effectiveness of novels like *The Brothers Karamazov* or *La Recherche du Temps Perdu*. Yet it is very difficult to discover in them any secret of technique which contributes materially to their effect. There is, in fact, nothing but their innate intensity. They consist of a duration of interest, and nothing more. Then turn to *The Awkward Age* with its carefully placed " lights ", its exacting objectivity, its suggestion of a geometrically contrived quincunx. One cannot resign *that* pleasure, *that* sense of definite pattern, of conscious fidelity to a discipline. Or we may take a more obvious example from the same author's work: *The Other House*. This novel was originally written as a play, but for very natural reasons James did not succeed as a playwright. So he turned this play into a novel, and as a novel it gains obviously and enormously from its dramatic substructure. Its unities, its situations, are composed "in space". Its intensities are static compositions. Yet it is a novel, and a very good novel too, and suffices to put Monsieur Thibaudet's theory in doubt. If we go back to *The Awkward Age*, a more significant performance, and contrast it with *The Brothers*

Karamazov, we are confronted with a dilemma. I do not pretend to resolve this dilemma. It is, perhaps, merely a statement of thesis and antithesis: the expression of mentalities diverse enough to be called positive and negative. Monsieur Thibaudet's theory has, it should be noted, certain Bergsonian affinities, and Bergson is merely the latest philosopher of Romanticism. The dramatic theory, on the other hand, is more reminiscent of Aristotle.

History. The temperamental novel suffers from its late entry into civilization. To tell a story is one of the oldest impulses of society, but it was a long time before that impulse took any notice of abstractions: of relations, mental and emotional complexities, moods and manners—all the stock-in-trade of the temperamental novelist. The temperamental novel—we may call it the modern novel—does not exist before Richardson, and does not exist in any of its essential subtlety until we reach Stendhal. It thus began its existence at a time when all other literary forms—poetry and drama—had for centuries been defined and had even outlived their possibilities of experiment. Perhaps this alone is a situation sufficient in itself to explain the rapid—too rapid—growth of the mere numerical units of the novel; though other equally plausible explanations can be found in the shifting of various economic and social factors—particularly in the mechanical possibilities of printing and distributing, the growth of the reading habit, and the education of a reading public. But so overwhelming was the demand on all putative novelists that they had no time to elaborate a *Poetics* for their art, and even the few solitaries who took their art seriously were swamped, as influences, by the thousands who merely wrote by instinct.

And then, if the novelists began to write by instinct, they continued to write by imitation; only in these later days have they recovered the old habit, but with a difference: they now write by instinct deliberately.

Analysis. The English tribute to Marcel Proust[1] was not rich in critical distinctions: it compared poorly with the corresponding volume published by *La Nouvelle Revue Française.* But among the generally vague appreciations there was a note by Conrad which showed at least a sense of direction. He wrote:

"The important thing is that whereas before we had analysis allied to creative art, great in poetic conception, in observation or in style, his is a creative art absolutely based on analysis. It is really more than that. He is a writer who has pushed analysis to the point when it becomes creative. All that crowd of personages in their infinite variety through all the gradations of the social scale are rendered visible to us by the force of analysis alone."

[1] *Marcel Proust, An English Tribute.* London, 1923.

The application of this passage depends on the meaning we attach to the word analysis; or rather, as to whether the word analysis, in its simple and accepted sense, is rightly used by Conrad in this connection. For is Proust's method really analytical? Is it not rather a process of extension? The so-called analysis begins with an image, or a statement, and then, by the method of association, other images or statements are conjured up and placed in relation to the object. Images for the sake of images, emotions and sentiments for their own sake: something dangerously analogous to mere verbalism. Such a method leads to some very interesting types of *poetry*, and is almost the distinctive method of the most original kind of modern poetry; and Proust is in this sense a very original poet.

But analysis, which is admittedly the particular business of the modern tradition in fiction, is something swifter, more clarifying. It is not the accretion of particulars so much as the selection of essentials. Analysis must work within a closely defined area; and the analyst must keep his eye on the object.

This is the whole difference, or the essential difference, between Proust and Henry James; the difference between "the terrible fluidity of self-revelation" and the precision of a disciplined writer.

Discipline. This word, like analysis, can be applied to our subject in various senses. There is the sense implied by Remy de Gourmont in his *Problème du Style*:

" Il n'y a pas telle ou telle sorte d'art; il n'y a pas d'un côté la science et de l'autre la littérature; il y a des cerveaux qui fonctionnent bien et des cerveaux qui fonctionnent mal."

This implies that the art of writing should be controlled by the same logical discipline that is essential to constructive thought. It implies the *ordonnance* of structure, of relation, and proportion; above all, it implies economy. But even Gourmont himself (who, great critic though he was, had an excessive regard for the place of sensibility in art) concludes his essay with these words:

" Si rien, en littérature, ne vit que par le style, c'est que les œuvres bien pensées sont toujours des œuvres bien écrites. Mais l'inverse n'est pas vrai: le style seul n'est rien. Il arrive même, car en esthétique comme en amour tout est possible, que le style, qui fait vivre un temps certaines œuvres, en fait périr d'autres prématurément. Cymodocée est morte étouffée sous sa trop riche et trop lourde robe.

" Le signe de l'homme dans l'œuvre intellectuelle, c'est la pensée. La pensée est l'homme même. Le style est la pensée même."

But it would be a mistake to translate " la pensée " in too limited a sense. Its implication is not at all, in this context, metaphysical or logical. Thought applied to character, which is its proper direction in the novel, resolves itself into something which had better be called moral. Such was the particular perception of Henry James, and this fact, more than anything else, endows him with qualities which give him the absolute dominance over all modern novelists. This moral perception is the animating energy of all his work, from its earliest full inception in *Roderick Hudson*, to its perfectly open expression in such obvious terms as *Madame de Mauves*, right unto its finest and subtlest and most significant statement in *The Ambassadors*.

This moral significance of the work of Henry James is naturally not the aspect to which, in all modesty, he could himself directly draw attention. But in many indirect ways he was always suggesting it: by his criticism of other novelists, by his attitude in life, and by many cryptic signs in the novels and tales themselves. There are two particular occasions on which he seems to indulge this need of self-revelation with more than ordinary emotional emphasis: one is in that rather fanciful image of Flaubert, in *Essays in London*:

"Let Flaubert be cited as one of the devotees and even, when people are fond of the word, as one of the martyrs of the plastic idea; but let him be still more considerately preserved and more fully presented as one of the most conspicuous of the faithless. For it was not that he went too far, it was on the contrary that he stopped too short. He hovered for ever at the public door, in the outer court, the splendour of which very properly beguiled him, and in which he seems still to stand as upright as a sentinel and as shapely as a statue. But that immobility and even that erectness were paid too dear. The shining arms were meant to carry further, the other doors were meant to open. He should at least have listened at the chamber of the soul. This would have floated him on a deeper tide; above all it would have calmed his nerves."

The other occasion is provided by the story of *The Figure in the Carpet*, where the sense of mystification was obvious enough to drag the rather poor thing into the limelight, but only to increase the irony of the situation—which was a general failure of perception—by the degree in which this blind ignorance became mere vulgar curiosity. No one, unless it is Mrs. Wharton, has fully realized this situation, or tried to express the abounding and increasing wonder of this master's work as it unfolds its firm perception of social values in character and action—values, too, of civilization and culture, all incorporated in the fundamental problem of good and evil, and envisaged in the urgency and peculiar aspect of modernity.

This is merely to indicate the central significance of the art of Henry James. There are other aspects more peculiar to the craft of fiction which cannot be even promulgated in these cursory notes: they are mainly questions of form and expression. On the question of form he was himself quite openly explicit, especially in the Prefaces to the definitive edition of the novels. A clear but scarcely a precise statement[1] of the problem of form as affecting the development of the novel was made by him in an essay on "The New Novel" as late as 1914 (reprinted in *Notes on Novelists*) and among his letters we have much vigorous and informal insistence on the subject; for example:

"Don't let anyone persuade you—there are plenty of ignorant and fatuous duffers to try to do it—that strenuous selection and comparison are not the very essence of art, and that Form *is* not substance to that degree that there is absolutely no substance without it. Form alone *takes*, and holds and preserves, substance—saves it from the welter of helpless verbiage that we swim in as in a sea of tasteless tepid pudding, and that makes one ashamed of an art capable of such degradations."[2]

Egoism. There is another passage, from the Preface to *The Ambassadors*, which I am tempted to quote, and then I have finished hurling this mandatory conception of a great writer in the way of a public who would rather take him for what, after all, he really is—a master of the art of amusement.

"Had I, meanwhile, made him at once hero and historian, endowed him with the romantic privilege of the 'first person'—the darkest abyss of romance this, inveterately, when enjoyed on the grand scale—variety, and many other queer

[1] "How can you say I do anything so foul and abject as to 'state'" (*Letters*, vol. ii, p. 254).

[2] *Ibid.*, p. 246.

matters as well, might have been smuggled in by the back door. Suffice it, to be brief, that the first person, in the long piece, is a form foredoomed to looseness, and that looseness, never much my affair, had never been so little so as on this particular occasion."

Since Henry James's time two novels have appeared which might by the unwary seem to dominate the tendencies of this "prodigious" form: I mean Marcel Proust's *A la Recherche du Temps Perdu* and the *Ulysses* of Mr. James Joyce. It is to be observed that both these ambitious renderings of the flow of life ignore the necessity imposed by Henry James on his work, and indulge in the looseness for which he had such an anxious dread. It is said that Proust's work will reveal, in its entirety, a sense of proportion and of architectonic unity not easily perceptible in the piecemeal form in which it has of necessity been issued to the public. A form of architecture of such elaborate detail would leave me sceptical if other reasons did not support the supposition of failure which follows from an acceptance of Henry James's criteria; these other reasons I will examine in another note. And of *Ulysses* it is said that it possesses an elaborate analogical structure having reference to the prototype of Homer. I am neither sufficiently impressed by the adequacy for modern sensibility of the formal qualities of Homer's epic, nor sufficiently convinced of the value of such an analogical method, to weigh this consideration much against the clearer and more definite conceptions promised by the formulas of Henry James. Form is not merely another aspect of style, for it reflects not so much the sensibility as the intelligence of the artist. I would never accuse either Proust or Joyce of a lack of sensibility; but their possession of orderly intelligence, in the sense given to it elsewhere in this volume, is more in doubt. They have genius, but irregular genius; and their works, whilst destined to be indicators of contemporary sensibility, are at the mercy of time to an extent not to be feared for the more regular and symmetrical genius of Henry James.

Expression. The tragedy of Henry James, the fault that, whilst not obscuring him from the patient few, yet divorces him from the instinctive understanding of the *illiterate* (the *educated* do not matter so much) is a certain defect of expression which developed only too rapidly as the psychological conditions of his life closed in upon him and enveloped him. This is not a subject which can be treated in a note; it is not a subject for which we have the necessary facts; but it is obvious to anyone with ordinary psychological perception that the tricks and mannerisms, the involved and parenthetical diction, and even the subtle illustration of his truly grand and tragic themes—these are the effects of a defeat in the development of his personal life. There is a terrible want, not of sensibility, but of actual and active participation in the life of the senses, which merely results, by an easily comprehensible law of compensation, in all the abortive rigmarole of his style.

The Sense of Values. It has been suggested that the positive quality of the art of Henry James is to be found in that sense of values, the presence of which is easily realized in his art, but only with difficulty analysed into its component elements. He had that particular perception of the interdependence but necessary relation of moral and aesthetic values for the want of which so much modern art has become defunct. It is not that the novel, or any other form of art, must be moralistic; the psychological basis of all aesthetic effects is obvious enough, and has no need of transcendental sanctions. But a work of art is the expression of a given personality and takes its colour and its life from this personality.[1] "There is one point at which the moral sense and the artistic sense lie very near together; that is in the light of the very obvious truth that the deepest quality of a work of art will always be the quality of the mind of the producer." So wrote Henry James himself, and these words are not only the finest justification of

[1] And yet the place of moral values in art is not to be confused with the question of the personal morals of the artist. It is possible that the necessity of moral values would be best appreciated by someone who did not himself possess them. The artist's sensibility registers his perceptions, and our only concern is that the mind of the artist is capable of organizing those perceptions into some intelligent conception of life.

his own nature and the nature of his art, but also the final test of all art whatsoever. It is the test which Monsieur Ramon Fernandez has applied with such admirable decisiveness to the art of Marcel Proust.[1] "Les objections que soulève l'œuvre de Proust, considérée comme analyse intégrale du cœur, comme révélatrice du fond de notre nature, peuvent être à mon avis réduites a deux essentielles: elle n'édifie point une hiérarchie des valeurs, et elle ne manifeste, de son debut à sa conclusion, aucun progrès spirituel." Monsieur Fernandez begins his essay with this very direct affirmation of precisely those qualities which we have seen desiderated by Henry James. I cannot here relate the various stages of psychological analysis and of dogmatic statement ("Le seul progrès effectif serait celui de l'intelligence, le seul perfectionnement non illusoire serait le perfectionnement de notre conscience intellectuelle") by which Monsieur Fernandez supports his case. It is sufficient to note that the essential defect of Proust is psychological, and therefore demonstrable without reference to the dogmatic affirmations which a positive critic is always ready to put in the place of the myth he has destroyed. It is a question of the relation of sensibility to intelligence, and of the tyranny, in Proust, of an evident passivity:

"Marcel Proust souffrait d'une hypertrophie de

[1] "La Garantie des Sentiments et les Intermittences du Cœur" (*La Nouvelle Revue Française*, no. 127, April 1924).

l'affectivité: or le plaisir et la douleur trop fortement ressentis détruisent l'ordre des choses et ramènent à eux les valeurs sentimentales par un subterfuge qu'il est aisé de concevoir. Par les résonances disproportionnées qu'ils savent tirer du corps ils donnent une fausse voix à l'âme, comme ces ventriloques qui font parler les spectateurs muet et surpris. Le patient de ces fortes décharges, trompé par son sens intime, et séduit par cette orchestration impérieuse, finit par croire qu'il vit, alors qu'il est vécu par les choses dont ses spasmes ne sont que les ondes transitoires; rien ne le détourne de l'erreur suprême qui consiste à prendre ses sensations pour des sentiments; et quand la vague affective se retire, ou qu'un accident quelconque en contrairie le déferlement, tout à coup il se sent nu, inutile et vidé jusqu'à ce qu'une autre vague le soulève et crée pour un instant le fantôme de son moi. Le plus grave est que la prépondérance des décharges affectives l'empêche de distinguer les choses les unes des autres par leur valeur, et par conséquent de distribuer sagement l'effort de son intelligence, puisque le parfum d'une rose et le parfum d'une âme lui créent pareillement un moi et justifient également son aversion ou son désir."

The distortion of reality which results from such a sensibility as Proust's is a sufficient objection to any purely formal or aesthetic judgement. But an abnormality of vision is not sufficient in itself to defeat our interest. The *interest* is there, our attention is held—but for how long? Even the contemporary reader begins to sicken in the close prison of an individual sensibility. The survival value, for remoter generations, is extremely problematical. One type of fiction lasts by virtue of its epical or energetic appeal: it involves only, or mainly, the faculty of visualization, which is common to all men; and such lengthy narratives as the *Odyssey* or *Don Quixote* in this way survive as narratives of progressive action. But a work of fiction that depends for its appeal on the creation of passive states of consciousness—either by the analysis of character or the building up of an emotional entity—such a work must pass from one generation to another with the least possible obstruction of material factors; it must be above the accidents of time. But this kind of superiority is only possessed by works of art which embody the utmost economy of construction and effectiveness of outline. The unity of the state of consciousness or of the emotional atmosphere must be apprehended directly and for its own sake. Elements of decoration, of documentation, of mere curiosity and aimless research into the moment of consciousness, of "becoming", entirely traverse and overwhelm the necessary impression of aesthetic unity. And without a unity, whether of action or of form, no work of art can possibly survive.

James Joyce. These remarks on the work of Proust apply in much the same manner to the work of James Joyce. But *Ulysses* does not altogether lack a sense of moral values; it is even dictated by such a sense. But it does lack a sense of intellectual progress—of the difference, that is to say, between the nature of our existence and the possibilities of that existence. It is an art deficient in aspiration; an art of the used and rejected remnants of life, a mortuary art. It is not an art of the truth, for, as Monsieur Fernandez has remarked in his essay on Proust, truth includes not only what man is, but also what he desires to be.

But Mr. Joyce is urged by a tremendous fury, a spleen which refuses the current coin of expression and drives him to a re-animation of words and syntax. In this sense Mr. Joyce is completely free, and the most inspiring of all modern prose writers. That liberation has in itself something approaching to a moral value: but it is not really moral because it is not associated with any manifest sympathy. It is merely an iridescence from which other writers will gather a suggestion for their living colours.

INDEX